NEW YORK STATE GRADE 4 ELEMENTARY-LEVEL SCIENCE TEST

Joyce Thornton Barry, M.S. Ed.

Kathleen Cahill, M.S. Ed.

BARRON'S

About the Authors

Joyce Thornton Barry is the Science Chairperson K–12 for the Plainview–Old Bethpage Central School District. She holds a B.S. in Biology, an M.S. in Special Education, and a Professional Diploma in School District Administration. During her more than 20 years as a science educator, she has developed inquiry-based science experiences for students of all academic abilities and levels, such as Preschool, Elementary, Secondary, and College. She has participated in writing questions and setting the scale scores for the NYSED Living Environment Regents. Joyce dedicates this book to her supportive husband Michael and wonderful children, Alanna and Brendan.

Kathleen Cahill is the Director of Science and Technology Education for the Wantagh Public Schools. She holds a B.S. in Biology and Psychology, an M.S. in Secondary Science Education, and a Professional Diploma in Educational Administration. During her more than 20 years as a science educator, she has worked with teachers and students at all levels to share with them her love of science. She is a member of the New York State Biology–Chemistry Professional Development Network, and has worked on curriculum development units for the University of Rochester Life Science Learning Center. Kathy dedicates this book to her family and friends who have encouraged her in this endeavor.

All inquiries should be addressed to:
Barron's Educational Series, Inc.
250 Wireless Boulevard
Hauppauge, New York 11788
www.barronseduc.com

ISBN-13: 978-0-7641-3734-1
ISBN-10: 0-7641-3734-4

ISSN 1936-136X

Date of Manufacture: May 2013
Manufactured by: B11R11, Robbinsille, NJ

Printed in the United States of America
9

CONTENTS

IMPORTANT NOTE: Barron's has made every effort to ensure the content of this book is accurate as of press time, but New York State exams are constantly changing. Be sure to consult **www.p12.nysed.gov/apda/ei/eigen.html** for all the latest New York State testing information. Regardless of the changes that may be announced after press time, this book will still provide a very strong framework for fourth-grade students preparing for the exam.

INTRODUCTION

This spring you will take an important test. It is called the New York State Grade 4 Elementary-Level Science Test. There is no need to worry about this test because you and your teachers have been preparing for this exam since you were in kindergarten. The test takes **two sessions** to complete. They are usually given on two different days.

1. **Performance Assessment** - You will enjoy this part of the test because you will be given an opportunity to show what you have learned about science by using different materials to complete scientific activities. There are three stations at which you will be asked to perform science experiments. You will be given 15 minutes at each station to complete the activities and answer questions about your findings.

   You will be asked to do the following:

   - Sort Objects
   - Observations
   - Measurement: length, mass, volume
   - Predictions
   - Magnetism
   - Electricity
   - Record Data
   - Comparisons
   - Interpret Data

2. **Written Test** - This part of the test has two parts. You will have as much time as you need to answer the questions to the best of your ability.

- Part I contains 30 multiple-choice questions
- Part II contains approximately 15 open-ended questions

The most important thing to do when taking any test is to read the questions carefully.

Note: The answer explanations to all Practice and Test Your Skills questions can be found in the Answer Key beginning on p. 201.

THE LIVING ENVIRONMENT

Chapter
1

LIVING VS. NONLIVING

Living things are both similar to and different from each other and from **nonliving things**. The world around us is made up of both living and nonliving things. Living things depend upon each other and the nonliving environment to survive.

Animals and plants are living things. They have basic needs (necessities) in order to survive. We often say that living things (**organisms**) are alive.

I. CLASSIFICATION OF LIVING THINGS

Animals need **air**, **water**, and **food** to live and survive.

- Animals take in air by breathing. They need **oxygen**, which is in the air. Oxygen allows the animal to make and use **energy**, which it needs to survive.
- Animals also need water to survive. Water is used to break down and move materials throughout the body.
- Animals cannot make their own food so they must eat to get **nutrients**. Nutrients are necessary for growth and energy.

Plants need air, water, nutrients, and light to live and survive.

- Plants take in air through their leaves. The type of air that plants take in and use is **carbon dioxide**. This is necessary for the plant to create food. Plants make their own food by a process called **photosynthesis**.
- Water is used by the plant to move materials up from the roots to make food.
- Nutrients from the soil enter the plant through its roots. Nutrients are necessary for the plant to survive.
- Light is one of the most important things for a plant. Light gives the plant the energy it needs to survive.

If the living organism does not get the air, water, food, nutrients, or light it needs to survive it will die.

Practice

A. List three things that you need to live and survive:

1. _____
2. _____
3. _____

B. Circle the items in the diagram below that are nonliving and place an "X" over those that are living.

C. Water helps living things survive by

a. bringing in gases.

b. keeping them clean.

c. creating food.

d. moving materials.

D. Air and water are necessary for _____ to survive.

a. plants

b. animals

c. both plants and animals

d. nonliving things

II. CLASSIFICATION OF NONLIVING THINGS

Nonliving things are all around us. They are present in nature or can be made by humans. They do not have a **life cycle**.

A rock is considered a nonliving thing; it exists in nature. A nonliving thing does not need anything to exist; it does not grow or reproduce and it is **not alive**.

A swing set is a nonliving thing that is man-made. Your desk, pencil, and paper are all nonliving things. They were made by humans but cannot change or grow on their own. Air and water are nonliving but are necessary for living things to live and survive.

Object	Living	Nonliving
Bench		
Grass		
Newspaper		
People		
Tree		

Practice

E. A mountain is a

   a. nonliving thing that occurs in nature.

   b. nonliving thing that is man-made.

   c. living thing that occurs in nature.

   d. living thing that is man-made.

F. Look at the drawing on the opposite page and place an "X" in the column of the table that represents each object.

G. List two nonliving things that all living things need to survive.

   1. _____

   2. _____

III. LIFE PROCESSES

All living things are able to go through certain life processes.

They can grow, take in nutrients, breathe, reproduce, eliminate waste, and die. These life processes are also known as the **requirements for life**.

Growth - Most animals are born as a smaller version of what an adult looks like. As they grow their bones get longer and bigger, they grow more hair, and are able to take care of themselves by getting food, shelter, and water. All living things grow and have a life cycle.

Some animals are born as one type of organism and as they grow they go into a changing stage called **metamorphosis**. Tadpoles change into frogs, caterpillars change into butterflies, and mealworms turn into beetles. This is their way of growing and changing.

Frog Eggs → Tadpole → Adult Frog

Plants can grow from a seed into a flower, tree, or bush. Plants reproduce by producing flowers and fruits that have seeds. The seeds then grow into plants. Other plants develop outgrowths that can grow into adult plants.

Life Cycle of a Flowering Plant

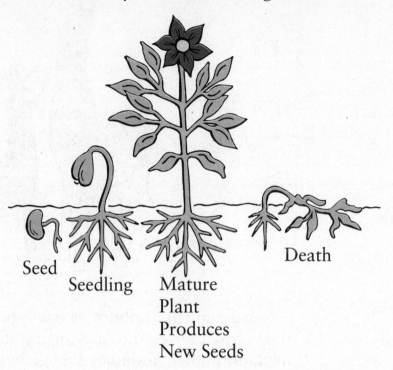

Seed

Seedling

Mature
Plant
Produces
New Seeds

Death

Nutrition - All living things need nutrients to survive. Animals take in food as a nutrient to give them energy and help them grow. Plants get their nutrients from the soil, which helps them grow and perform photosynthesis. Photosynthesis is the process by which plants make their own food.

Breathing - All living things do some type of breathing. Most animals take in oxygen through their mouths. Fish breathe through gills. Both **inhale** (take in) oxygen, which is used to create energy. Oxygen is found in the air all around us. Animals **exhale** (give off) carbon dioxide, which is used by plants. Plants take in carbon dioxide and give off oxygen.

Reproduction - All living things are able to produce **offspring**; we usually call them babies. Some offspring are born looking like their parents.

Some offspring are born as one form and change over time into an adult form.

Eliminating Waste - All living things must be able to get rid of the solid waste that they produce. Animals take in food to get nutrients. After their bodies have used the nutritious parts of the food they must get rid of the leftover material that they cannot use. All animals get rid of this solid waste after passing food through their digestive system. The waste leaves the body in the form of **feces**. This waste, when mixed into the soil, can be very helpful to growing plants.

Animals get rid of their gaseous waste by exhaling carbon dioxide through their mouth and nose. Plants get rid of chemical waste through their roots. Plants get rid of gaseous waste through their leaves in the form of oxygen.

Practice

H. The life process where animal bones get longer and bigger is called

   a. growth.

   b. reproduction.

   c. breathing.

   d. nutrition.

I. Frogs and butterflies look very different from when they are born. The changes they go through are called

   a. skipping.

   b. metamorphosis.

   c. fading.

   d. breathing.

J. Explain why living things need nutrients to survive.

_____

_____

K. Oxygen is given off by _____ and taken in by _____.

   a. animals, animals

   b. plants, animals

   c. animals, plants

   d. plants, plants

L. What materials make up an animal's fecal waste (feces)?

_____

TEST YOUR SKILLS

1. Note if the item is living or nonliving.

_____

_____

_____

_____

_____

_____

2. List two things plants need to grow and survive.

    1. _____

    2. _____

3. Nonliving things

    a. grow in a garden.

    b. take in foods.

    c. can be man-made.

    d. need air to survive.

4. In order to live and survive, animals need

    a. air, food, and water.

    b. only light.

    c. only air and food.

    d. only air and water.

5. _____ are able to make their own food by a process called photosynthesis.

6. A seed growing into a plant is a form of what life process? _____

7. Explain how living things need nonliving things to survive.

_____

_____

Chapter 2

PLANTS

Plants are living organisms. Plants require air, water, nutrients, and light in order to live and survive.

Plants contain little green particles called **chloroplasts**, which are made up of **chlorophyll**. Plants are the only living organism that can make its own food. Chlorophyll is used for photosynthesis, the process by which plants make food.

Other living organisms depend on plants to survive.

Plants provide animals with food and gases (oxygen) that their bodies need to grow, breathe, and make energy.

Practice

A. In order for a plant to live and survive, what do they require?

    a. food and water

    b. air and light

    c. air, water, light, and nutrients

    d. light only

B. Chlorophyll is used for _____.

C. What kind of plants and or plant products do you like to eat? Give at least three examples.

    1. _____

    2. _____

    3. _____

D. What are some ways that an animal might use plants to survive? Give at least two examples.

    1. _____

    2. _____

I. PHOTOSYNTHESIS

Photosynthesis is a process by which plants make their own food and give off oxygen and water that they are not using. The food made by the plant is a form of sugar called **glucose**. Oxygen is a gas that is needed by many animals in order to survive. Humans inhale (breathe in) oxygen and exhale (breathe out) carbon dioxide.

Water + Carbon Dioxide → Energy from Sunlight →
Glucose + Oxygen

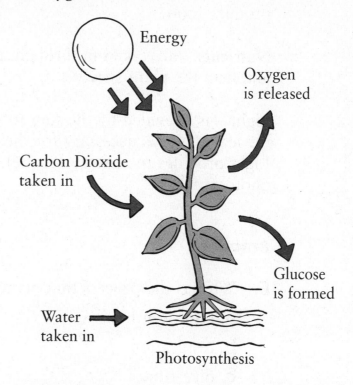

Photosynthesis

Air – The leaves of the plants take in carbon dioxide from
the environment. They give off oxygen, which animals
need to survive.

Photosynthesis

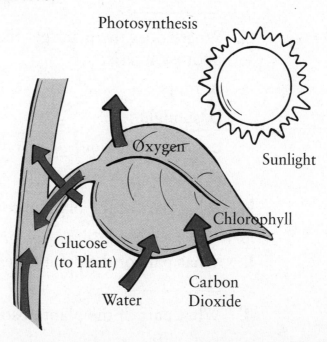

Water – is taken in from the environment through the roots in the ground and is necessary for the plant to produce food.

Nutrients – are taken in through the roots from the soil and help the plant survive.

Light – is provided by the sun. It is **absorbed** (taken in) by the leaves and is necessary for the plant to produce food. Light provides the energy for the entire process of photosynthesis.

Practice

E. What is the process that plants use to make food?

    a. photosynthesis

    b. respiration

    c. digestion

    d. propagation

F. When plants make food, they give off _____ and _____.

G. Where does the plant get the energy to go through photosynthesis?

    a. roots

    b. sunlight

    c. carbon dioxide

    d. leaves

H. What part of the plant absorbs carbon dioxide?

_____

I. What part of the plant takes in (absorbs) water?

_____

J. What part of the plant absorbs sunlight? _____

II. PLANT STRUCTURE

There are four major parts of a plant: roots, stem, leaves, and flower.

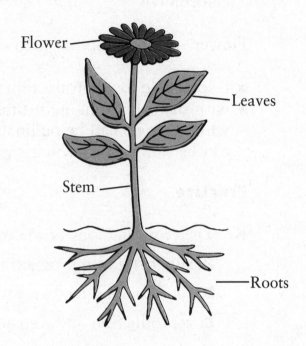

Flower

Leaves

Stem

Roots

Each part of a plant has a specific job (**function**).

Roots – grow underground

■ anchor the plant in the soil
■ absorb water and nutrients from the soil into the plant

Stem, stalk, or trunk – extends from the roots up to the leaves and flower

■ pathway of water and nutrients from roots to leaves and flower
■ supports and holds up the plant
■ pathway for **transporting** (carrying) water and nutrients
■ transports extra food (glucose) made in the leaves to the roots to be stored for later use.

Leaves – extend from the stem

- food-making **factory** of the plant
- makes food using water, sunlight, nutrients, and chlorophyll

Flower – found atop the stem or stalk

- responsible for reproduction
- with the help of animals (insects and birds), rain, and wind, flowers can be **pollinated** (**fertilized**) so that seeds can be formed that will grow into new plants

Practice

K. The two functions of the roots are

    a. support and reproduction.

    b. food-making factory and anchor.

    c. reproduction and transport.

    d. anchor and absorb.

L. Describe the job (role) of the stem in photosynthesis.

_____

_____

M. What part of the plant do we call the food-making factory and why?

_____

_____

III. REPRODUCTION

The flower is the reproductive part of the plant. Flowers are usually bright colors and have nice scents for a reason. These colors and smells attract birds and insects to visit them and help with the reproduction process.

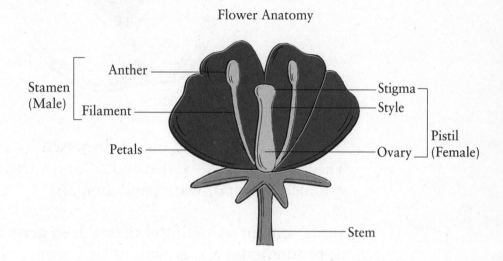

Flower Anatomy

In the flower there are male and female reproductive parts.

- The **male** organ of the flower is called the **stamen** (containing **pollen**).
- The **female** organ of the flower is called the **pistil** (containing **eggs**).

When plants reproduce, the offspring has characteristics similar to the parents. Seeds are formed when cells from the male and female parts of the plant combine. Seeds grow in the center of a flower and continue to develop there after the petals fall off the plant. If the seed surroundings swell up they can form a fruit. All fruits have seeds. Some have one big seed, called the pit, like a peach. Some fruits have a few seeds, like an apple. Some fruits have many little seeds, like a kiwi.

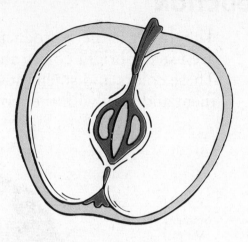

Seeds can be spread out or **dispersed** by the plant itself. The seeds can also be distributed in a variety of ways that can include wind, water, and animals.

Seeds contain stored food that aids in **germination** (**sprouting**) and the growth of new young plants.

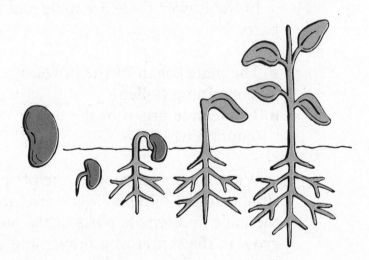

Practice

N. How does the flower help the plant reproduce?

_____

_____

O. What are some common fruits? (Give at least three
examples.)

1. _____

2. _____

3. _____

P. How does a fruit develop?

_____

_____

Q. Seeds are sometimes found inside a fruit. How can a
fruit spread its seeds?

_____

_____

IV. ADAPTATIONS

Adaptation is an organism's ability to adjust to its
surroundings. Some plant adaptations might include:

- Thorns on stems to protect the plant from being eaten
- Large leaves to increase surface area for photosynthesis
- Colored or patterned leaves and/or flowers in order to
  blend into the environment
- Roots grow longer to reach the water supply

- Leaves and stems develop tough outer coatings to protect the plant from the environment
- Stems become thicker to prevent water loss

Practice

Choose the letter of the kind of tree you would find in the following environments.

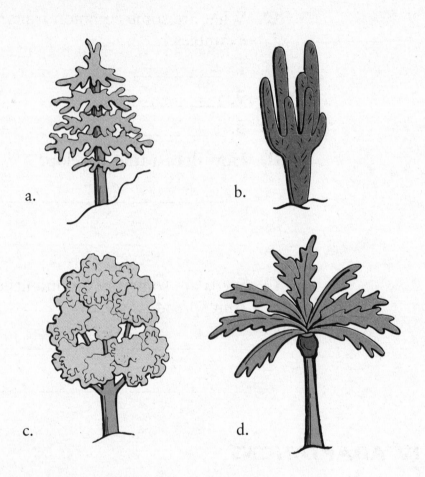

a.

b.

c.

d.

R. In the desert: _____

S. In the tropics: _____

T. In a New York City park: _____

U. In the mountains: _____

V. Give one adaptation a plant can have and explain how it helps it to survive.

_____

_____

V. LIFE CYCLES

Plants have life cycles that may include beginning of life, development into an adult, reproduction as an adult, and eventually death. The length of time from the beginning of the plant to its death is called its **life span**. Each kind of plant goes through its own stages of growth and development, which includes seed, young plant (or **seedling**), and mature plant.

Growth is the process by which plants increase in size.

Life Cycle of a Flowering Plant

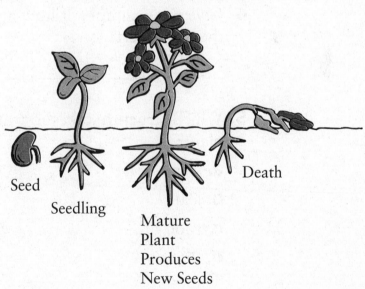

Seed

Seedling

Death

Mature
Plant
Produces
New Seeds

TEST YOUR SKILLS

1. What substances does a plant need to survive?

_____

_____

2. How does a plant reproduce?

_____

_____

3. Where in a plant would you find a fruit?

_____

_____

4. Give one example of how a plant adapts to survive in the dry desert.

_____

5. Which structure takes in water and nutrients for a plant?

a. stem

b. leaf

c. root

d. flower

6. Which is *not* a common method by which seeds are dispersed from a plant?

   a. wind

   b. water

   c. insects

   d. airplane

7. Which is an example of a typical life cycle of a plant?

   a. seedling → seed → plant

   b. seed → seedling → plant

   c. seedling → plant → seed

   d. plant → seedling → seed

8. Which is an example of a plant responding to a change in its environment?

   a. bees flying around flowers

   b. rain falling on soil

   c. roses growing different colors

   d. leaves falling off trees in fall

9. Which structure is the part of the plant responsible for reproduction?

   a. flower

   b stem

   c. leaf

   d. root

10. One function of the stem of a plant is to

   a. make food for the plant.

   b. help the plant reproduce.

   c. contain seeds.

   d. provide support for the plant.

11. The process by which a plant increases in size is known as

a. breathing.

b. growth.

c. reproduction.

d. elimination of waste.

Chapter 3

ANIMALS

Animals are living organisms. Animals require air, water, and food in order to live and survive. All animals grow, take in nutrients, breathe, reproduce, eliminate waste, and die. Each animal has different structures that serve different functions for growth, survival, and reproduction.

STRUCTURE AND FUNCTION

All animals are made up of **cells** that have specific functions (jobs). Groups of cells make up **tissues**. Muscles and skin are examples of tissues. Groups of tissues working together are called **organs**; the lungs are an organ in the body. Different organs working together are called **organ systems**. These organ systems work together to make up the organism.

Cells → Tissues → Organs → Systems → Organisms

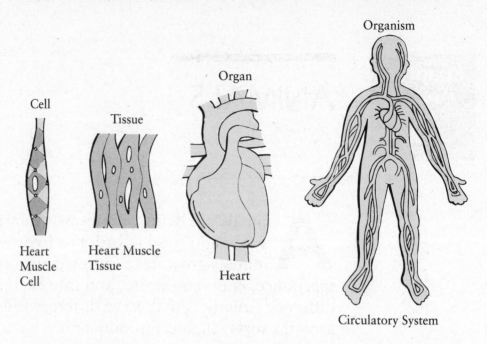

Circulatory System

Each organ system has a specific function that helps the organism to survive. The body systems work like a machine and each system works to help the animal grow, create energy, and survive.

I. ORGAN SYSTEMS

Digestive System – All animals need to take in food, water, and nutrients (vitamins and minerals) to survive. They take food into their mouth, where the **teeth** and **tongue** break up the food into smaller pieces so that it can be swallowed. The food then goes through a tube called the **esophagus** to the **stomach** where it is broken down more. The digested food then moves into the **intestine** where the nutrients are absorbed into the blood. Any undigested food exits the body as feces through the **anus**.

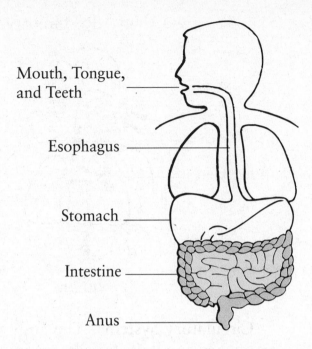

Mouth, Tongue, and Teeth

Esophagus

Stomach

Intestine

Anus

Ingestion – food is taken into the body
Digestion – nutrients are taken into the body
Egestion – undigested food leaves the body

Respiratory System – All animals need to take in oxygen in order to survive. We do this by breathing. Animals take in air, which contains oxygen, through the **nose**. After we inhale the air it moves through a tube called the **trachea** to the **lungs**. In the lungs, the oxygen enters the blood so that the oxygen is carried throughout the body. All cells need oxygen to survive. After the cells use the oxygen the blood carries the waste, carbon dioxide, back to the lungs. The lungs send the carbon dioxide out of the body when we exhale. The **diaphragm** is a muscle that moves up and down as we inhale and exhale and helps the lungs take in and let out air.

Respiratory System

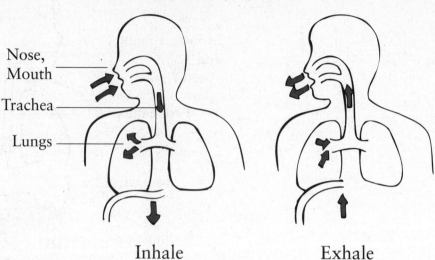

Nose, Mouth

Trachea

Lungs

Inhale   Exhale

Circulatory System – The body must get nutrients and oxygen to all of its cells, tissues, and organs; it does this by **circulating** blood throughout the body. The blood carries the nutrients through tubes called **vessels**. The blood is circulated (carried) all over the body because of a strong muscle that continuously pumps the blood called the **heart**.

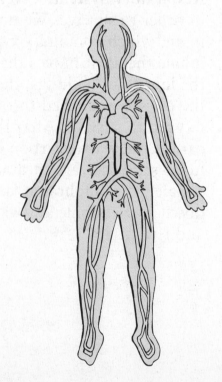

When you put your fingertips against the inside of your wrist you can feel the blood pulsing through your vessels.

Urinary System – After the blood carries nutrients and oxygen throughout the body we need to get rid of the **chemical waste**. The blood takes the chemical waste and excess water to the **kidneys** where it is collected and sent to the **bladder** until the body excretes it as **urine**.

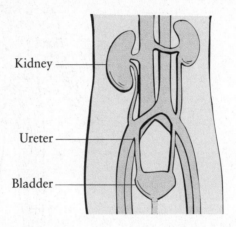

Kidney

Ureter

Bladder

Locomotion System – Animals need to move around to find shelter and food. They do this by moving muscles and bones. The **skeleton** provides support and protects the body's organs.

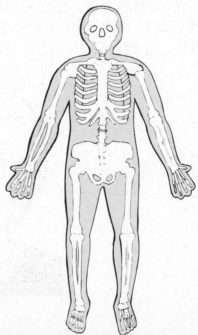

Nervous System – All animals need to **sense** their surroundings, respond to environmental changes, know where and how to find food, care for their young, and many other things. They do all of this with their **brain** and **nerves**.

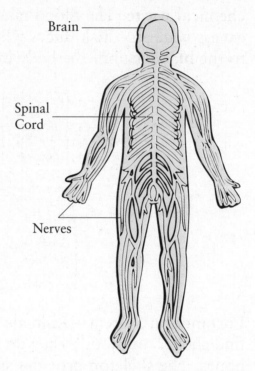

Humans have five senses: **taste, touch, smell, sight,** and **hearing**. The senses tell the organism all that is happening around them.

We hear with our **ears**. The vibrations from sound move tiny bones in our ears which send a message through the **auditory nerve** to the brain so that we understand what is being heard.

We taste with our **tongue**. There are tiny sensors on the tongue called **taste buds** that identify different tastes such as sweet, sour, bitter, and tart. The taste buds send information to the brain so that we can decide if we like or dislike the taste.

We see with our **eyes**. The eyes take in light through the lenses and transmit the shapes and images through the **optic nerve** to the brain.

We touch with our **fingers** and **skin**. All over the skin there are tiny spots that feel things and transmit texture, temperature, and other characteristics to the brain by way of the nerves.

We smell with our **nose**. Tiny hairs and nerves in our nose sense different smells and send them to the brain so that we can decide if it is a familiar scent or a new one.

Practice

A. Use the word bank and match the function with each organ system. Word Bank: movement, take in nutrients, breathing, senses, eliminate chemical waste, pumps blood

Digestive: _____

Respiratory: _____

Circulatory: _____

Locomotion: _____

Urinary: _____

Nervous: _____

B. The five senses are controlled by the _____ system.

   a. locomotion

   b. digestive

   c. nervous

   d. circulatory

C. What do animals need to survive?

   a. air, water, and food

   b. water, clothes, and shoes

   c. water only

   d. food and water

D. Cells → _____ → organs → organ systems → organisms

   a. nerves

   b. tissues

   c. heart

   d. atoms

E. Which organ helps in digestion and respiration?

   a. kidney

   b. heart

   c. mouth

   d. ears

F. Which system is responsible for getting rid of chemical waste and water?

   a. digestive

   b. urinary

   c. locomotion

   d. circulatory

G. Which system protects the organs and provides structure for the body?

a. digestive

b. urinary

c. respiratory

d. locomotion

II. VARIATIONS

All animals have different structures that have different jobs or functions to help with growth, survival, and reproduction.

Animals have different ways of movement. Birds use their **wings,** fish use their **fins,** and others use their **legs.** Animals need to move so that they can find a safe place for shelter, find food, and escape predators (**enemies**).

Lobsters and crabs protect themselves with their **claws,** turtles have **shells,** porcupines have **spines,** birds use their **feathers,** and others have **fur** or **scales** to help protect them from predators.

Some animals are able to change the color of their body covering to that of their surroundings. We call this **camouflage,** which helps protect the animal from enemies. Think of a lion's golden fur, which helps it blend into the desert landscape. Chameleons are lizards that can change colors based on the color of their surroundings. On the sand it will turn a tan color and on grass it will turn green to allow it to hide from predators.

Some animals protect themselves by sending out special sounds or smells, which is another type of **defense mechanism.** These smells and sounds can attract other animals so that they can mate or they can help them fight an enemy. Skunks are able to give off a very foul smell when in danger. This is how they protect themselves.

III. ANIMAL RESPONSES TO THE ENVIRONMENT

Behavior is the way that organisms respond to changes in their environment or to a stimulus.

Humans shiver when it is cold and by doing so we create more heat in an attempt to warm our bodies. In the hot weather our bodies sweat (perspiration), bringing water to our skin. When air brushes across our wet skin, it cools down our body.

When we get nervous, scared, or upset our body responds by increasing our heart rate; we breathe faster and begin to sweat. This is how our body prepares itself for whatever danger may be coming.

SEASONAL CHANGES

Some animal behaviors are influenced by environmental conditions. These behaviors may include: nest building, hibernating, hunting, migrating, and communicating.

Many animals are able to change their body with the seasons. We wear winter coats, gloves, and hats when the weather is cold. Some animals grow thicker fur in the winter and shed it in the warmer months; this helps to regulate their body heat. Other animals change their amount of **body fat** with the seasons. Body fat is a form of stored energy and helps animals get through long periods of time with little food. Some animals gather food in preparation for the long winter; squirrels collect acorns.

Some animals live a very different life in the warm weather than in the cold weather. Some animals hibernate during the winter months; their bodies slow down and go into a **dormant** (inactive) state. Bears hibernate but before doing so they eat a great deal of food to increase their body fat. They are able to go for a long period of time with little food and will sleep until the cold winter months pass.

Moving to a warmer climate in the cold months is another way some animals deal with changes in the weather. This is called migration. Birds are known for flying south in the winter to avoid the cold months.

Practice

H. All animals have different structures that have different jobs or functions to help in _____, _____ and _____.

I. List and describe two ways that animals respond to changes in their environment, such as seasonal changes.

    1. _____

    2. _____

J. When animals move to a warmer climate to avoid the change in seasons, we call this

    a. hibernation.

    b. camouflage.

    c. perspiration.

    d. migration.

K. Some animals prepare for the long winter by storing food and going dormant. This is called

    a. hibernation.

    b. migration.

    c. fleecing.

    d. reservation.

L. Explain the differences between how dogs, birds, and fish move around.

_____

_____

M. Why do some animals have claws, spines, shells, or give off a smell?

    a. migration.

    b. hibernation.

    c. seasonal change.

    d. defense mechanism.

N. Animals that change color or are of a color similar to their environment can _____ themselves so that they cannot be easily seen.

IV. ADAPTATIONS

Individual organisms and species **change** over long periods of time. These changes (**adaptations**) depend on the environment. Adaptations are passed from one generation to the next so that the species can survive and thrive. The saying, **"survival of the fittest"**, means that those who are best adapted will survive over those who are not.

One example of how organisms have adapted to their environment is the fish. Because fish live in the water and need to breathe, they developed **gills**. Gills are slits in the sides of their body that allow the fish to get oxygen from the water while swimming.

Camels are able to go for long periods of time with little water; this makes them the best type of animal to live in the desert. Cactus plants can also go for long periods of time with little water, which is why they survive in the desert.

Look at the similarities and differences between animals' arms and/or wings. Depending on how the organism lives, their arm and/or wing adapted to help it survive.

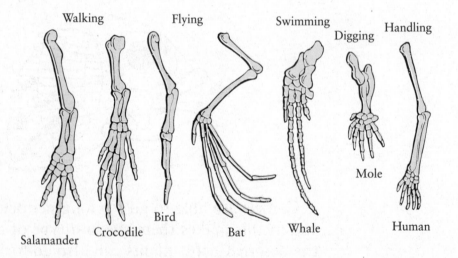

A bird's **beak** functions like human lips and teeth. A beak helps the bird capture and take in food. Compare the various beaks shown below and think about what type of food each bird eats. The shape, strength, and design of the beak varies depending on whether it is a bird of prey, a seed-eater, or a fish-eater.

Elephants have long trunks that enable them to grab food and drink water. They also have very large ear flaps that help them hear. Because of their size, elephants move very slowly, so having good hearing helps protect them from predators.

All organisms have **variations,** and because of these variations, individuals of a species may have an advantage in surviving and reproducing. **Diversity** is the many different types of animals within the same species. There are many different breeds of dogs but there are variations within the same breed. You could have three beagles that look similar but their markings are different.

Practice

O. A giraffe's long neck helps it eat leaves that are high on trees. This trait can be considered a(an)

a. adaptation.

b. difficulty.

c. camouflage.

d. migration.

P. Explain why a pelican's beak is helpful to the bird.

Q. In what type of environment do animals with gills live?

a. desert

b. forest

c. prairie

d. water

R. Give two examples of how animals' limbs adapt to their environments.

1. _____

2. _____

S. Cats have distinct colors and patterns that make them look different from other cats. This is an example of

a. adaptation.

b. camouflage.

c. diversity.

d. hibernation.

V. REPRODUCTION/LIFE CYCLES

All living things go through different stages in its life. They are born, grow (develop), have babies (offspring), and die. This is called the **continuity of life** or **life cycle**. When an organism has an offspring (baby) it is called **reproduction**. As they grow and change over time it is called **development**.

Living things must reproduce and have babies so that their species will continue. If they are not able to reproduce, their species will become **extinct**. Extinction is when the species no longer exists, such as the dinosaurs.

All living things have specific patterns of reproduction, growth, and development that are called **stages** in its life cycle.

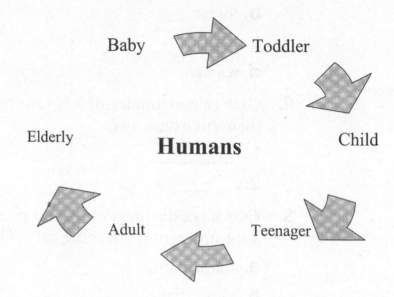

Baby → Toddler → Child → Teenager → Adult → Elderly

Life cycle stages go in a certain order and occur throughout the life span of the organism. The characteristics of the cycle of life vary from organism to organism. You may have had a pet or witnessed some of the following organisms' life cycles.

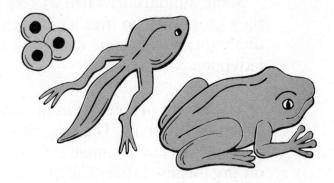

Eggs → Tadpole → Adult Frog

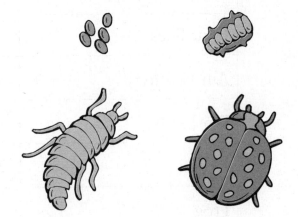

Eggs → Larva → Pupa → Adult LadyBug

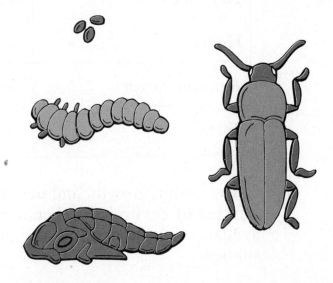

Eggs → Larva → Pupa → Adult Beetle

Some animals are born as one type of organism and as they grow they go into a changing stage called **metamorphosis**. Some examples are the frog, beetle, and ladybug.

The length of time from an animal's birth to its death is called its life span. The type of environment they live in and various environmental factors can have a direct effect on organisms. Life spans of different animals vary.

Animal	Life span (average)
Fruit Flies	72 hours
Ant (worker)	6 months
Worker Bee	1 year
Rabbit	9 years
Frog	10 years
Elephant	70 years
Human	79 years
Amazon Parrot	80 years
Turtle	100 years

The health, growth, and development of organisms are affected by environmental conditions such as the availability of food, air, water, space, shelter, heat, and sunlight.

Growth is the process by which plants and animals increase in size. All living things are constantly going through some form of growth and repair. When young the overall body is growing and developing. This is evident by how tall or big the organism grows. As an organism moves into an adult stage of life they continue to grow. This is proven by how their hair and nails continue to grow and need to be maintained. When an animal breaks a bone it is able to heal over time. This healing is done by the body growing new bone cells to repair the break.

Think about when you may have cut yourself and after a short period of time the cut healed. Usually your body can heal from a cut without any scar remaining. This happens because your body is always growing and making new skin cells.

Practice

T. Describe the major stages in the life cycle of humans.

_____

_____

U. The life cycle continues through _____ and _____.

V. During which phase of the frog's life span are they able to swim with the help of a tail?

  a. egg

  b. tadpole

  c. larva

  d. adult frog

W. The length of time from an animal's birth until death is called its

  a. life span.

  b. instinct.

  c. life cycle.

  d. development.

X. Describe any similarities and differences between the life cycles of the ladybug and the frog.

_____

_____

TEST YOUR SKILLS

1. This is a diagram of which organ system?

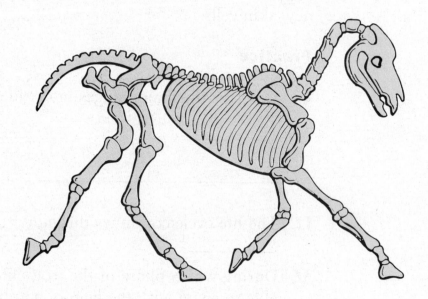

a. circulatory

b. respiratory

c. digestive

d. locomotion

2. A defense mechanism is a way in which animals

a. protect themselves.

b. find mates.

c. avoid the seasons.

d. adapt.

3. How do rabbits grow into adults?

   a. They absorb sunlight.

   b. They have bones that grow.

   c. They go through metamorphosis.

   d. They shed their skin for new skin.

4. Choose the correct life cycle.

   a. Baby → elderly → adult → child

   b. Child → elderly → baby → adult

   c. Baby → child → adult → elderly

   d. Elderly → adult → child → baby

5. What is most important for the survival of a species?

   a. respiration

   b. reproduction

   c. locomotion

   d. circulation

6. During which season of the year would a bear's fur be thickest?

   a. summer

   b. spring

   c. winter

   d. fall

7. Proof of how animals have adapted for survival in their environment is shown in this photo of a dolphin flipper and a human arm. Explain how they have both adapted.

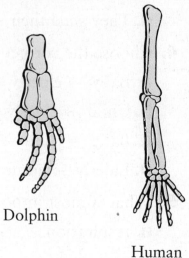

Dolphin

Human

_____

_____

8. The brain and spinal cord are part of which system?

   a. nervous

   b. respiratory

   c. circulatory

   d. digestive

9. List four senses that can be used to observe an orange.

   1. _____

   2. _____

   3. _____

   4. _____

<table>
<tr><td>**Chapter**
4</td><td># GENETICS</td></tr>
</table>

H ave you ever noticed that some children look like their parents and some may also look like their grandparents? How does this happen?

All living things get the information their body needs from their parents. This information is called **traits**. A trait could be the color of your hair, skin, and eyes, your height, and the shape of your face, ears, and nose. These are all **characteristics** (traits) that you are born with. When a trait is passed from parent to child we say that it is **inherited**. Inheritance is passing characteristics from parent to child.

Genetics is the branch of science that studies how hereditary information is passed from one generation to the next generation in a family.

FAMILY TREE

A family tree is a chart that shows a family's relatives over time. In the family tree chart shown below, the grandparents are the first generation, the parents are the second generation, and the children are the third generation.

A **pedigree chart** shows each level of a family tree in a chart format. Lines and boxes connect parents and children from one level to the next, as shown below.

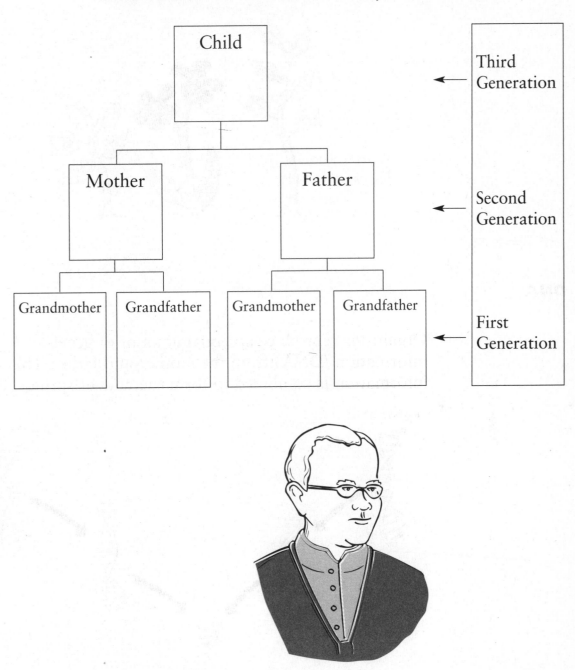

Gregor Mendel was a scientist who is known as "the father of genetics." Mendel researched how pea plants pass on their traits from one generation of plant to the next. Inherited traits for a plant are flower color, leaf shape, seed shape and color, and overall plant height.

DNA

Organisms reproduce an equal amount of genetic information (**DNA**) from the mother and father. This information is combined to form the new offspring.

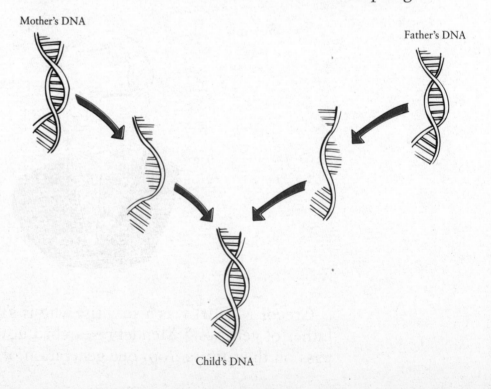

Practice

A. Organisms pass on characteristics from parent to offspring. This is called

    a. linking.

    b. inheritance.

    c. owning.

    d. sharing.

B. Characteristics that are passed from a parent to child are called

    a. traits.

    b. marking.

    c. DNA.

    d. items.

C. A baby can inherit a trait from a

    a. teacher.

    b. neighbor.

    c. parent.

    d. friend.

D. List four traits that can be inherited.

    1. _____

    2. _____

    3. _____

    4. _____

E. Draw your family tree and circle each generation.

Family Tree

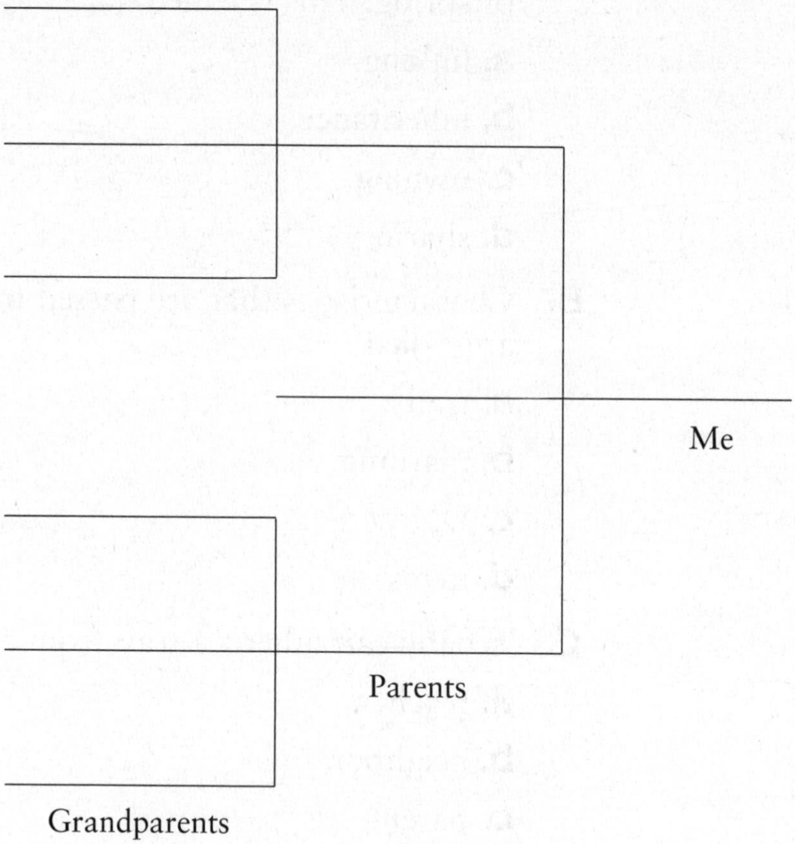

Me

Parents

Grandparents

F. Organisms reproduce DNA from the _____ combined to form the genetic information for the new offspring.

GENES

Traits are carried on structures called **genes**. Genes are found in all cells. Genetic information is organized on very tiny structures in the cell called DNA (**DeoxyriboNucleic Acid**). DNA is a bundle of chemicals that are considered the map for all living things. Every organism's DNA is different. Just as you have your own fingerprint, you also have your own DNA. DNA tells all living things what it should look like.

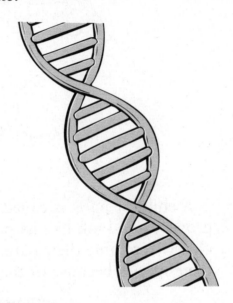

DNA looks like a twisted ladder. Each step of the ladder controls different traits. Each **strand** of DNA contains hundreds of pieces of information. There are many strands of DNA in our body. The number of DNA strands (**chromosomes**) an organism has is the same for all members of a **species**. For example, humans have 46 chromosomes and a fruit fly has only 8 chromosomes.

Many organisms look very similar to other organisms because they may be from the same species. When organisms are of the same species they can mate and produce an offspring like themselves.

A child or baby is called an offspring. An offspring grows up to look like its parents. Plants and animals closely resemble their parents and other individuals in their species because of their DNA.

Animals reproduce their own kind. They may have different markings but you can tell that they are related.

- rabbits have rabbits
- cats have kittens
- goldfish have guppies
- frogs have tadpoles
- dogs have puppies

An organism can only have an offspring from their own species; dogs cannot have kittens and rabbits cannot have guppies.

Practice

G. Explain how DNA is like a fingerprint.

_____

_____

H. Genes are found in

  a. hair.

  b. cells.

  c. air.

  d. teeth.

I. What does DNA look like?

_____

J. Genes carry

  a. traits.

  b. markings.

  c. stories.

  d. items.

K. _____ and _____ closely resemble their parents and other individuals in their species because of DNA.

   a. plants, rocks

   b. animals, rocks

   c. rocks, insects

   d. plants, animals

L. List three traits that animals and plants get from their parents.

   1. _____

   2. _____

   3. _____

M. Draw a line to match the parent with the offspring.

ENVIRONMENTAL TRAITS

Some characteristics come from living in the environment and cannot be inherited by the next generation. For example, if you fall and get a deep cut that leaves a scar, you would not pass the scar to your offspring.

Do you know how to jump rope, ride a bike, tap dance, read, play an instrument, or sing? These are not traits from your parents; these are called learned or acquired behaviors. You cannot pass these traits to your offspring through your genes. You could teach them how to do each behavior but they are not born knowing how to do them.

Answer the following questions:

Do you have freckles? _____
Is your hair straight or curly? _____
What color is your hair? _____
What color are your eyes? _____
What is the color of your skin? _____
Can you roll your tongue? _____

These are all called traits that we inherit from our birth parents.

Practice

N. DNA is found in the _____ of our body.

O. DNA is responsible for _____.

P. All _____ things have DNA.

Q. Is rolling your tongue inherited or acquired?

_____

R. Which characteristic is *not* inherited?

a. having curly hair

b. eye color

c. scars

d. blood type

TEST YOUR SKILLS

1. What are the bundles of chemicals in our body called that control what we look like?

   a. cells

   b. genes

   c. DNA

   d. filaments

2. What part of DNA contains hundreds of pieces of information?

   a. tissues

   b. chromosomes

   c. muscles

   d. blood cells

3. Where do our genes come from and what determines hair, eye, and skin color?

   a. memory cells

   b. blood cells

   c. medicine

   d. parents' DNA (parents' genes)

4. Where is DNA found in our bodies?

   a. genes

   b. bones

   c. cells

   d. brain

5. Mark an "X" if the trait is inherited or acquired.

Trait	Inherited	Acquired
Hair color		
Scar on elbow		
Riding a bike		
Shape of earlobe		
Color of flower		
Height		

6. Explain why organisms resemble their parents from generation to generation.

_____

_____

7. Which family does *not* look related to this mother and child?

a.

b.

c.

d.

8. A giraffe will have a baby
   a. elephant.
   b. dog.
   c. cat.
   d. giraffe.

9. The flowers in the first generation

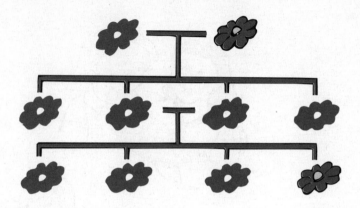

a. all look like both parents.

b. are all the color of one parent.

c. are all white like one parent.

d. do not look like the parents.

<table>
<tr><td>Chapter
5</td><td></td></tr>
</table>

GOOD HEALTH

Your body is like a very delicate machine that needs to be cared for to work and feel its best. In order for humans to grow, have energy, and be healthy they need to **eat healthy foods, exercise,** and **get regular rest.**

Being healthy also includes **good health habits.** Hand washing and **personal cleanliness** are necessary to prevent disease and infection.

There are many **germs** that can be transmitted from touching things and then placing your hands by your face. This is why you need to wash your hands often to remove any harmful germs. The body needs to be cleaned regularly to prevent germs and **bacteria** from growing and making us sick.

Brushing your teeth in the morning and before going to bed is another important part of having good health. Our teeth build up food throughout the day and overnight while we sleep. Brushing our teeth removes the food and helps keep them strong.

Covering your mouth when you cough or sneeze is another way to prevent your germs from passing to someone else.

If you get a cut it must be cleaned to prevent any bacteria from creating an **infection (disease)**. After the wound is cleaned it should be covered with a bandage to reduce the chance of getting infected.

You have only one chance to live a healthy life style. The best way to do this, in addition to eating healthfully, exercising, and getting rest is to **avoid** (do not take or try) **harmful substances.**

Smoking cigarettes, tobacco, or illegal drugs is very harmful to your body. When a person smokes there are chemicals released by the tobacco that enter the lungs. Because the lungs have to work harder to remove the chemicals, the body has to work harder to get the air needed to survive. The chemicals from smoking can also cause very serious diseases such as lung cancer. Smoking can also cause skin and teeth to turn an unhealthy color.

Drinking **alcohol** and/or taking **illicit** (not prescribed) **drugs** are also very harmful to your body. In order for alcohol and drugs to get out of your body the blood takes it to the liver, which is the organ that cleans the blood. The liver has to work harder to remove these foreign substances. As a result, your body may develop some serious illnesses.

Eating a **balanced diet** is one of the most important steps toward having good heath. It is important to take in the proper foods and nutrients everyday so that your body can grow, have energy, and repair itself. A balanced diet includes:

- **Grains** – bread, rice, pasta, cereal
- **Vegetables** – lettuce, broccoli, carrots, cucumbers
- **Fruits** – apples, bananas, oranges, grapes, pears
- **Milk** – cheese, yogurt, cream, dairy
- **Meats and Beans** – hamburger, chicken, eggs, tuna, nuts
- **Oils and Sweets** – butter, oil, sugars (in very limited amounts)

The **MyPyramid** is an easy way to plan the foods you are going to eat. Each part of the pyramid represents the proper amounts of each type of food that will help you stay healthy. Also, you should keep in mind that regular exercise is necessary to live a healthy lifestyle.

MyPyramid

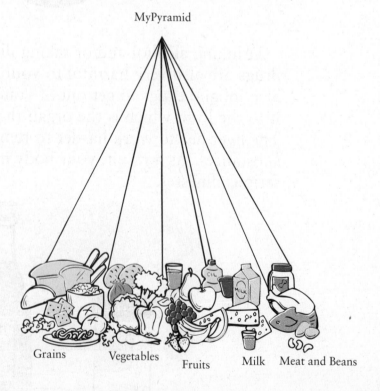

Grains   Vegetables   Fruits   Milk   Meat and Beans

When we run, jump, walk, play sports, or ride our bike we are exercising. Not only is it fun, but it is healthy for our bodies. When we exercise our body is working hard and moving the nutrients, water, and air throughout our body.

Getting enough rest is also an important part of living a healthy life. Our bodies need time to rest and recover from our busy day. While we sleep our body gives the cells time to grow and repair. When we get a good night's sleep we are able to better concentrate in school and find it easier to complete our work.

TEST YOUR SKILLS

1. In order for humans to grow and be healthy they need to _____, _____ and _____.

2. To avoid getting germs and illnesses from other people you should

   a. eat bread everyday.

   b. exercise weekly.

   c. wash your hands frequently.

   d. go to bed on time.

3. Which is a harmful substance?

   a. salad

   b. candy

   c. fruit

   d. cigarette

4. The food pyramid shows us

   a. how not to eat.

   b. which foods make a balanced diet.

   c. that we do not need to exercise.

   d. which foods to avoid.

5. An example of a poor health habit is

   a. eating candy for dinner.

   b. washing your hands after using the bathroom.

   c. playing at the park every afternoon.

   d. getting 8 hours of sleep at night.

Chapter 6

ECOLOGY

Ecology is the science that studies the **relationships** between organisms and their environments. These interconnected relationships are called **ecosystems**. An ecosystem is a community of all the living and nonliving parts of an environment.

Plants and animals depend on each other and the nonliving environment for survival. Living things need specific resources for survival such as air, food, and water.

While plants are able to make their own food by photosynthesis they need sunlight and water to do so. Plants also take in carbon dioxide from the environment and return oxygen to the air for animals to use. **Green plants** are called **producers** because they provide the basic food supply for themselves and animals.

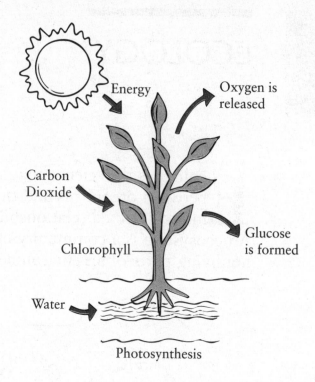

Photosynthesis

I. THE SUN AS ENERGY

The sun is the ultimate source of energy for all life and physical cycles on Earth. The sun's energy is transferred on Earth from plants to animals through the **food chain.**

Plants and animals interact in a number of ways that affect their survival. The survival of plants and animals varies in response to their particular environment. Provided there are enough resources for plants and animals they can survive in a successful (balanced) ecosystem community for long periods of time. The U.S. National Park Service is committed to preserving, protecting, and sharing the beauty of successful ecosystems. These protected areas are all over the United

States in deserts, forests, prairies, tropical areas, and arctic regions.

Individuals in a species may compete with each other for food, mates, space, water, and shelter within their environment.

Problems arise when the balance between the organisms and the available resources and space changes. Building homes, stores, factories, growing food crops, and pollution are some causes of ecosystem failure. As the physical environment changes over time, plants and animals change and so do the relationships within the ecosystem.

An organism's **pattern of behavior** is related to the nature of that organism's environment. This includes the kinds and numbers of other organisms present, the availability of food and other resources, and the physical characteristics of the environment.

Changes in the weather, too much rainfall, and severe cold or heat affect plants and animals. When there are environmental changes, some plants and animals survive, reproduce, and increase in number, while others die or move to new locations. This can have a major impact on the resources available; there may not be enough food or shelter.

Another example of an environmental change would be when there is a **natural disaster** such as a flood or fire. Some plants and animals are able to survive the changes while others may not.

II. FOOD CHAIN/FOOD WEB

Many things in our living environment go through cycles. All animals depend on plants either as a direct source of food and energy or because plants are food for another animal that they eat. Some animals (predators) eat other animals (**prey**). In the photo below, the cat is considered a predator and the fish is its prey.

Animals that eat plants for food may in turn become food for other animals. This sequence is called a **food chain**. There are three terms used in a food chain:

▪ **Producer** – living things that change the sun's energy to make their own food. Green plants do this by photosynthesis.

■ **Consumer** – living things that feed on others.
  ■ Primary (1ˢᵗ) consumer: eats the producers (plants)
  ■ Secondary (2ⁿᵈ) consumer: eats the primary consumer
  ■ Tertiary (3ʳᵈ) consumer: eats the secondary consumer
■ **Decomposer** – living things that break down dead organisms and recycle their nutrients into the soil. They help in plant growth.

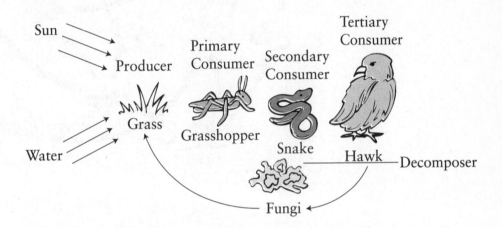

Some food chains crisscross and create a food web. They can be simple:

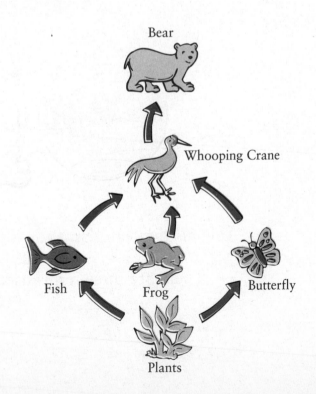

Or complex:

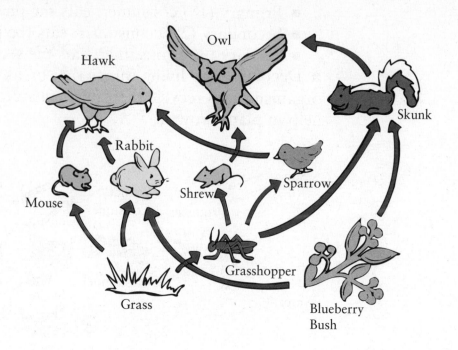

TEST YOUR SKILLS

1. The ___sun___ is the ultimate source of energy for all life and physical cycles on Earth.

Questions 2–5 relate to the diagram below:

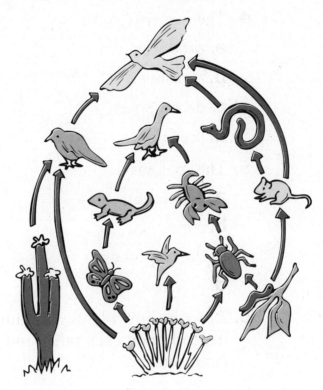

2. This diagram represents a(an)

   a. food web.

   b. ecosystem.

   c. food chain.

   d. decomposer.

3. The cactus is a

   a. producer.

   b. consumer.

   c. decomposer.

   d. predator.

4. The butterfly is a

   a. producer.

   b. consumer.

   c. decomposer.

   d. predator.

5. The snake is a

   a. producer.

   b. consumer.

   c. decomposer.

   d. predator.

6. Describe how plants and animals, including humans, depend upon each other and the nonliving environment.

_____

_____

Questions 7–9 relate to the diagram above.

7. Create a food chain using animals that you see in the diagram.

8. Identify a predator: _____

9. Identify a prey: _____

Observe the data in the table about animal reproduction.

Animal	Where Animal Lives	Number of Young Produced	Number of Young That Survive	Parental Care	No Parental Care
Clam	water	1,000,000	30		X
Falcon	land	5	2	X	
Horse	land	1	1	X	
Oyster	water	750,000	100		X
Salamander	land	100	8		X
Snake	land	35	3	X	
Spider	land	100	10	X	
Whale	water	1	1	X	

10. Explain how the environment and behavior of the organisms have an effect on their success in reproduction.

_____

_____

Chapter 7

HUMANS AND THEIR ENVIRONMENT

Human decisions and activities have had a major impact on the physical and living environments.

Humans are dependent upon the environment for food, shelter, and energy. Humans can live in many different environments. Some people live in very cold regions; others live in tropical areas where it can get very warm. Human's can live in areas with forests, prairies, deserts, or at the beach.

Humans use **resources** from the environment to create shelters and energy. By using materials that are found naturally in the environment humans must be responsible and make sure that they do not create problems for nature. Humans use wood to build homes, which comes from trees. Cutting down too many trees has resulted in many forest animals no longer having homes.

Humans also use materials found in nature to create energy. We use **fossil fuels** to make gasoline so that we can drive cars and trucks and fly planes. Fossil fuels like oil and natural gas are used to heat our homes and power factories to make items that we purchase. It can take thousands of years for certain fossil fuels to be created. Humans must learn how to conserve our planet's natural resources.

Humans depend on natural and constructed environments. The way that humans treat the environment has a large effect on the survival of all living and nonliving things.

As humans build homes, stores, and communities they displace the animals that live in those areas. The animals have to move to new areas. If they find new homes, the animals could have difficulty finding food, could be in danger of predators, or might not adapt to the new environment. If they are unsuccessful in their new location, they may die. If organisms in a species are not able to reproduce, that species may become extinct. As humans construct new homes and buildings they change the landscape of the nonliving environment. Floods can result from altering the flow of water in the environment.

Humans have also changed the environment by **cultivating** (growing) **crops** and **raising animals**. Humans need food to survive and since the human population increases in size everyday there is a greater demand for food. For there to be enough food, farmers plant and harvest grain, wheat, corn, fruits, and vegetables. Animals are raised on farms for human **consumption** (to eat).

In addition to food, shelter, and energy, humans **manufacture** (produce) goods that make life more comfortable. Factories are built and materials are taken from the environment to create many different products.

Humans developed various means of **transportation** so that they could live in one place and bring food, energy, and other goods to them rather than living at the site where they are made. While it is nice to have cars, planes, and trains for transportation, these machines give off gases that are not helpful to the atmosphere.

Building shelters, using energy, manufacturing goods, and the various forms of transportation are some of the ways humans have created pollution. Pollution is found in the air, on the land, and in the water.

Humans have changed their environment by developing communities in areas where living things had to struggle to survive. When a new community is built in the desert, humans may bring in plants that are not familiar to that environment. Watering their imported lawns increases the moisture in the dry air. This can change the air quality and lead to pollution.

Humans can help the environment in many ways:

- Feeding animals that have lost their natural resources due to the development of stores and homes.
- Cleaning litter from beaches, parks, and forests.
- Recycling and reusing papers, plastics, and metals to reduce the amount of waste in landfills.

Recycle

- Using appliances that conserve energy (**energy efficient**).
- Creating new clean forms of energy to conserve fossil fuels.

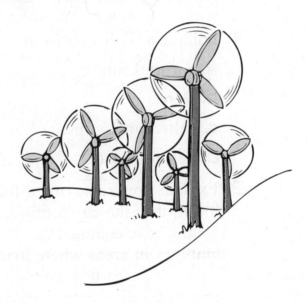

TEST YOUR SKILLS

1. Humans are dependent upon their environment for
   a. food, shelter, and energy.
   b. food and energy.
   c. food and shelter.
   d. energy and shelter.

2. Cars and trucks create

　a. energy that grows food.

　b. gases that are harmful to the atmosphere.

　c. gases that are helpful to the atmosphere.

　d. energy that creates gasoline.

3. Describe two ways that humans can help save their environment.

_____

_____

4. Pollution is created from

　a. harmful sounds.

　b. water.

　c. cultivating crops.

　d. harmful gases.

5. Explain how removing a forest to build homes can be harmful to the environment.

_____

_____

Unit 2

PHYSICAL SETTING

Chapter 8

MATTER

Matter is anything that has **mass** and takes up space. Mass is the amount of material present in an object. To measure mass scientists use a balance. **Volume** is defined as the amount of space an object takes up. To measure liquid volume scientists use a graduated cylinder. To measure the volume of a solid scientists use a ruler. Think of this book; it has mass as well as volume, therefore it is considered matter.

I. PHASES OF MATTER

Matter exists in three phases: **solid, liquid,** and **gas.** Solids have a definite shape and volume. Liquids take the shape of the container they are placed in and have a definite volume. Gases take the shape and volume of whatever container they occupy.

The simplest way to observe matter is to use your senses: sight, sound, taste, touch, and hearing. In addition to their senses, scientists often use **tools** and/or **instruments** to observe matter. Some tools include:

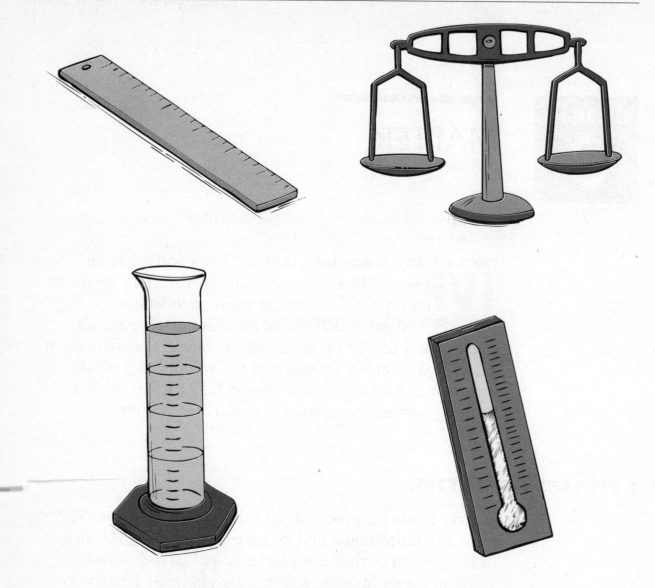

- ▪ Ruler – measures length
- ▪ Balance – measures mass
- ▪ Thermometer – measures temperature
- ▪ Graduated Cylinder – measures volume

Practice

A. What phases of matter are present in a glass of water that contains ice cubes?

_____

_____

B. Give an example of how our senses can identify matter.

_____

C. What tool/instrument would you use to measure the volume of this book?

_____

D. What tool/instrument would you use to measure the volume of milk used in a recipe to make pudding?

_____

II. PROPERTIES OF MATTER

Properties of matter can be considered **physical** or **chemical**.

Physical properties are those that can be observed and/or measured without changing the object. Physical properties include: color, hardness, odor, sound, taste, texture, and size.

Chemical properties are those that involve a change in the object. An example of a chemical property would be rusting.

CLASSIFICATION

Scientists often classify or organize different objects based on their physical properties.

Practice

E. What physical properties does this book have?

_____

F. Give an example of a chemical property.

_____

G. How would you classify the following list of groceries?

_____

_____

_____

_____

milk, apple juice, bread, chocolate chip cookies, oranges, lettuce, tomatoes, chicken noodle soup, pretzels, pork chops, eggs, American cheese, butter, shampoo, dishwasher detergent, soap, toothpaste, paper towels

III. CHANGES TO MATTER

Just as we can describe physical and chemical properties of matter we can describe the **physical and chemical changes** to matter.

Physical changes are those that involve changing one or more of the physical properties of matter. Consider a piece of notebook paper. What are some of the physical properties of the paper? We can describe the paper in terms of its color (white) and its size (21 centimeters wide and 27 centimeters long).

How can we change the paper in order to give it different properties but still consider it to be paper? We can rip the paper into little pieces. We can color the paper using crayons or markers. We can fold the paper into a smaller size.

Practice

H. Describe the physical properties of a pencil. Then, describe any physical changes that you could make to the pencil.

_____

_____

Chemical changes involve changing the composition of an object, resulting in entirely different properties.

Consider again our piece of notebook paper. We have seen how we can change a physical property of the paper, but still have it remain as paper.

How might we change the paper chemically? One way to change the paper would be to burn it. The white sheet of paper would become a pile of black ashes. The ashes are chemically different from the paper so this is considered a chemical change.

TEST YOUR SKILLS

1. Which instrument would a scientist use to measure the volume of a liquid?

   a. balance

   b. meter stick

   c. graduated cylinder

   d. thermometer

2. Which is an example of a chemical property?

   a. color

   b. rusting

   c. size

   d. texture

3. In which phase of matter do the particles have the most definite shape?

   a. gas

   b. liquid

   c. solid

   d. None of these.

4. Which is an example of using your senses to make an observation?

   a. using a ruler to measure the length of this paper

   b. using a balance to find the mass of your shoe

   c. using your eyes to see that a banana is yellow

   d. using a thermometer to measure the temperature outside

5. Which tool is matched to the object that it measures?

    a. balance – mass

    b. ruler – temperature

    c. graduated cylinder – mass

    d. thermometer – volume

6. Which is *not* an example of a chemical change?

    a. rusting of a bicycle

    b. burning of paper

    c. souring of milk

    d. melting of ice

7. Which phase of matter will take the shape of a closed container?

    a. gas

    b. liquid

    c. solid

    d. All of the above.

Chapter 9

ENERGY

Energy is the ability to do **work**. Work involves the changing of an object's position; moving up and down or from side to side. Without energy no work can be done. Think about going a whole day at school without eating. You would feel tired and not want to do anything. It would be because you have no energy. Energy for humans comes from the foods we eat. Food is converted to energy so that we can work and play.

Energy can be classified in a number of ways. An object could have **potential energy**, which is **stored** or **kinetic** energy, meaning that the object is in motion while using its energy. A rock at the top of a hill that is standing still has potential energy. If you give that rock a push and it begins to move up the hill, the potential energy is changed to kinetic energy, allowing the rock to move.

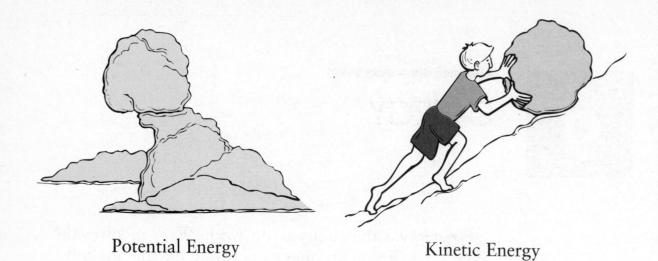

Potential Energy   Kinetic Energy

Practice

Classify the following as either kinetic or potential energy.

A. Parked car: _____

B. Bike rolling downhill: _____

C. Plane flying: _____

I. FORMS

Energy exists in many forms. Heat, electric, sound, chemical, mechanical, and light are all examples of different forms of energy.

- Heat – is the energy that gives us warmth. We can get heat energy from the sun.
- Electric – energy that allows us to turn on lights, ring doorbells, and so on.
- Sound – energy (noise) we hear when matter vibrates and the particles in the matter hit each other.
- Chemical – energy that is released when a chemical reaction takes place.
- Mechanical – energy produced when two objects move together.

■ Light – energy given off from a light source such as the sun or a light bulb.

Practice

Which form of energy is present in each of the following?

    D. Snowball melting in your hand: _____

    E. Turning on a radio: _____

    F. Banging a drum: _____

II. TRANSFERRING ENERGY

Energy can be transferred from one place to another and one object to another. Have you ever put a metal spoon in a pot that is being heated on the stove and then tried to touch the spoon? It gets hot. The heat from the pot is transferred to the metal spoon. If you were to put a wooden spoon in the same pot and then tried to touch it, the wooden spoon would not be hot. Why? Some materials transfer energy better than others. Examples of some forms of energy transfer are:

■ Mechanical – energy exerted by one object can push or pull another object.
■ Heat – can be transferred from one object to another object.
■ Magnetism – can be caused in some kinds of materials by a magnet.
■ Light – can be reflected from one object to another.
■ Sound – can be reflected from an object, causing an echo.

ENERGY/MATTER INTERACTIONS

In everyday life different forms of energy interact with matter. Much of this interaction results in energy changing from one form to another. Examples of interactions and conversions (changes) include:

■ Light energy to electrical energy in a solar calculator.

■ Mechanical energy to sound energy by clapping your hands together.

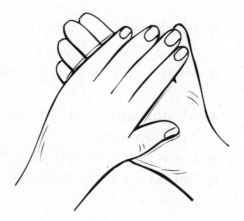

■ Electrical energy to sound energy in a door buzzer.

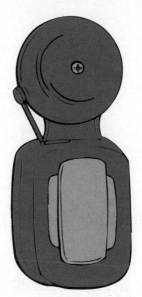

■ Mechanical energy to sound energy by playing a musical instrument.

▪ Chemical energy to electric energy in a battery.

Some other changes in energy include:

Form of Energy	Object	Energy Changes to:
mechanical	bicycle brakes	heat
	piano	sound
heat	tea kettle	sound
	flame	light
electrical	electric food mixer	mechanical
	radio speaker	sound
chemical	battery	electrical
	gasoline engine	mechanical
magnetic	magnetic door latch	mechanical
light	solar path lights	electrical

Energy can move from one object to another through different materials and through space. Some materials allow energy to be transferred more easily than others. For example, some metal objects allow heat and electricity to transfer better than do plastic or rubber objects. Iron and steel are more magnetic than wood or plastic. Light energy travels in straight paths through space. Light energy can move through glass much better than through paper.

Practice

Identify the energy changes in each of the following examples.

G. Pounding a fist on a table:

_____ to _____

H. Drying clothes in a clothes dryer:

_____ to _____

I. Battery:

_____ to _____

J. Playing a guitar:

_____ to _____

K. Blender:

_____ to _____

L. Car engine:

_____ to _____

III. ELECTRICITY

Electricity is one form of energy. Electrical energy results from positive and negative charges. A complete circuit allows electrical energy to flow. The amount of energy transferred during a flow of electrical energy depends on the energy source and the properties of the object.

Electricity powers many objects in our homes: television, radio, lights, computer, and other appliances. Electricity travels in a path called a circuit. A **simple circuit** generally involves a battery, or other source of electrons, wires through which the energy can flow, and the object that needs the energy to work, such as a light bulb. The circuit or path must be complete in order for the object to work. This is an example of a simple circuit:

One end of a wire is attached to a battery and the other end is attached to the base of the light bulb. From the light bulb there is another wire that runs back to the battery. When all the wires are attached, the bulb will give off light. When one of the wires is not attached, as in the diagram below, the circuit will not be complete and the bulb will not give off light.

TEST YOUR SKILLS

1. A ball is rolling down a hill. What type of energy does the ball have?

   a. potential

   b. chemical

   c. solar

   d. kinetic

2. Energy from the sun is called

   a. solar energy.

   b. sound energy.

   c. chemical energy.

   d. mechanical energy.

3. The energy transformation that occurs when you ring a doorbell is

   a. sound to light.

   b. electrical to sound.

   c. mechanical to heat.

   d. electrical to chemical.

4. Energy of motion is _____ energy.

5. Stored energy is called _____ energy.

Chapter

10

FORCES

A force is a **push** or **pull**. A force is what makes it possible to change the position of an object. A force can also be used to change the direction that an object is moving. The amount of force put on an object will determine how far and fast the object will move.

The weight of the object will also effect how far and fast it will move. Think about moving a box across a wood floor. If the box were empty and you gave it a push it would easily move across the floor. If the same box were full of marbles you would need more force to move it across the floor.

Friction is a force that provides resistance whenever two surfaces are in contact. The box pushed across the floor will eventually stop because of the force, or friction, the floor has on the box. The amount of friction that an object encounters depends on its smoothness. The smoother the surface, the less friction against an object, so the faster it will move. Skiers and surfers often apply wax to their skis and boards in order to make them smoother so they will glide along the surface of the snow or water faster.

Friction is also the force exerted by brakes on a bicycle or car in order to stop.

Take the same box from the previous diagram. What would happen if we were to try and push the box along the sand?

I. MAGNETISM

Another type of force is magnetism. A magnet is an object that attracts metals. The magnet works because the forces in it are all moving in the same direction, resulting in two different poles (ends). The space around the magnet is called the magnetic field. If you were to place a magnet under a piece of paper and sprinkle iron filings on the paper you would be able to see the magnetic field of the magnet.

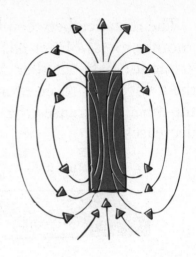

.The different poles of a magnet are attracted to one another. The poles are labeled north and south. If you were to take two magnets, the north end of one magnet would be attracted to the south end of the other.

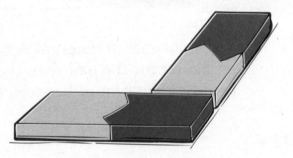

If, however, you were to try and put the two north ends of two different magnets together you would feel the force that causes the magnets to be **repelled** (pushed away) from one another.

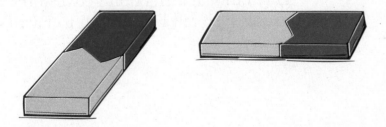

The distance between two magnets or a magnet and another metal object has an effect on the force of attraction. The smaller the distance between the objects, the greater the force of attraction. As the distance between the objects increases the magnetic force of attraction decreases.

Diagram A

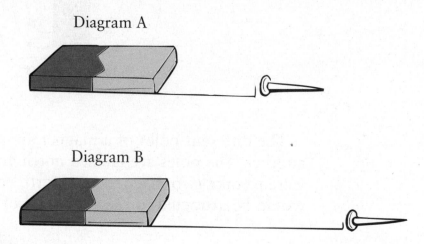

Diagram B

The magnet in diagram A has a greater force of attraction for the nail than the magnet in diagram B because the distance between the two objects is smaller.

II. GRAVITY

Gravity is also a force that acts on objects here on Earth. Gravity is the force that pulls an object toward the center of the Earth. It is gravity that keeps everything from flying away. If an object is thrown into the air, the force used will only allow it to travel a certain distance before the gravitational attraction between the object and the Earth causes it to fall back down to Earth's surface.

III. SIMPLE MACHINES

In the previous chapter we learned about work and energy. Mechanical energy is the energy produced when two objects move together. We have also learned that in order to do work an object must move and that a force is a push or pull. In our everyday lives we exert force to do work. Often the force we need in order to do the work is too much for one person and we need help. When this happens we use tools, or machines, to help us do work. **Simple machines** are tools with very few parts that help us work. There are a variety of simple machines:

■ Lever – a flat structure that is placed on a fixed point. The lever can assist in moving an object that is too heavy such as a big weight, or can assist in opening an object such as a paint can. The seesaw in a playground is also considered a lever.

■ Inclined Plane – a ramp that extends from one level to another. A wheelchair ramp into your school is an example of an inclined plane.

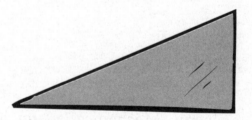

■ **Pulley** – composed of a wheel with a piece of rope or chain around it. Pulleys are used to lift objects. By pulling down on one end the opposite end is raised. A pulley is used to raise the flag up the flagpole at your school each day.

B

A

Pulling down on the rope at side A will cause the box on the end of the rope at side B to be raised.

■ **Wheel and Axle** – involves a wheel turning on a straight bar or axle. Examples of this type of machine are a door knob and the wheel on a wheelbarrow.

▪ **Wedge** – a type of inclined plane that can be forced into another object. The blade of an ax is considered to be a wedge.

▪ **Screw** – another type of inclined plane that is wrapped around a cylinder. By turning the screw you insert it into another object.

TEST YOUR SKILLS

1. Which of the following shows an inclined plane?

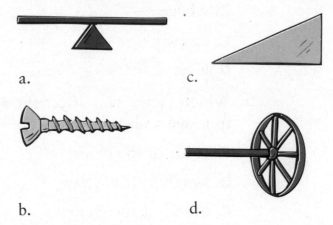

a.

c.

b.

d.

2. A force that slows down or stops the motion of a bicycle is

a. magnetism.

b. friction.

c. heat.

d. sound.

3. Matthew gets around in a wheelchair. Which of the following would be the easiest for him to climb?

a. a staircase

b. a steep hill

c. a ramp with a low incline

d. a ramp with a steep incline

4. The seesaw in a playground is an example of which type of simple machine?

  a. pulley

  b. wedge

  c. screw

  d. lever

5. Which factor will affect the amount of force necessary to move a chair across a room?

  a. color of the chair

  b. weight of the chair

  c. brand of the chair

  d. age of the chair

6. Which force acts to bring objects toward the Earth?

  a. friction

  b. work

  c. gravity

  d. magnetism

7. An object is placed on a table. A magnet is slowly moved toward the object. The object moves away from the magnet. The object is most likely a(an)

  a. copper coin.

  b. piece of glass.

  c. iron nail.

  d. magnet.

8. Amanda found a wooden box in her grandfather's garage. The top was nailed shut. What type of simple machine should Amanda use to open the box?

   a. lever

   b. pulley

   c. wheel and axle

   d. inclined plane

9. If an object moves toward a magnet, what can be said about the object?

   a. It is repelled by the magnet.

   b. It is attracted to the magnet.

   c. It is not a nail.

   d. It is a sticky substance.

10. A push or pull is called a _____.

11. When two objects slide over one another _____ can occur.

Use the following chart to answer questions 12–14.

The chart below lists some objects and shows whether a bar magnet picks up the object.

Object	Picked Up By Magnet
Staple	Yes
Rubber Eraser	No
Iron Nail	Yes
Crayon	No
Pin	Yes

12. List the objects that were attracted to the magnet.

    1. _____

    2. _____

    3. _____

13. What conclusion can be drawn from the chart about magnets?

_____

_____

14. Name another object that would be attracted to a magnet based on the information in the chart.

_____

15. Based on the diagram below, what will happen as magnet A is moved closer to magnet B?

      A   B

Chapter 11

ASTRONOMY

There are a number of different objects, called **celestial objects**, that appear in the sky each day and night. The **sun, stars, moon, planets,** and **comets** are all celestial objects. The apparent movement of these objects gives us an indication of the passage of time. The sun, moon, and certain stars can be seen everyday and night in our sky. We see different planets throughout the year because of the motion of the Earth and the movement of the planets around the sun.

I. TIME/SEASONS

The sun is considered the center of our solar system and all objects move around the sun. But the sun appears to "rise" and "set" each day. This is not because of the motion of the sun but rather the motion of the Earth. The Earth **rotates,** or spins, on its axis once every 24 hours. This rotation is what results in day and night on Earth. It is the rotation of the Earth that makes the sun appear to move through the sky during the day, rising in the east and setting in the west.

We measure time on Earth based on both the rotation of the Earth on its axis and its **revolution** around the sun. The passage of time in different units is based on the smallest unit being a second.

1 minute = 60 seconds
1 hour = 60 minutes
1 day = 24 hours
1 month = approximately 30 or 31 days
1 year = 12 months or 365 days

As the Earth revolves around the sun, its position changes and the amount of sunlight received by Earth also changes. The Earth is divided into two halves or **hemispheres**; the **equator** being the dividing line. Anything north of the equator is in the northern hemisphere and anything south of the equator is in the southern hemisphere.

The Earth is tilted on its axis; as a result, one part of the Earth is always pointed toward the sun. Because of the tilt and the Earth's position around the sun during its revolution the Earth experiences four distinct seasons: winter, spring, summer, and fall. In the northern hemisphere, where New York State is located, the seasons are divided as follows:

Winter: December 22 to March 19
Spring: March 20 to June 19
Summer: June 20 to September 21
Fall: September 22 to December 22

Each season has its distinct weather conditions, which will be discussed in the next chapter.

II. MOON PHASES

The moon is a satellite of the Earth. This means that the moon orbits (moves around) the Earth in a path. The movement of the moon around the Earth is called revolution. The moon does not give off its own light. We see the moon in the sky because it reflects light from the sun. Half of the moon's surface is continually lit by reflected sunlight. The moon makes a complete orbit around the Earth once every 29½ days. This means that it takes approximately one month for the moon to completely revolve around the Earth. Because of the moon's movement and the reflected light from the sun we see different portions of the moon at different times during the 29½ days. The different portions of the moon that we see are called phases. There are five phases of the moon:

Full – a complete circle of the moon is visible
Gibbous – almost a complete circle of the moon is visible

Quarter – half a circle of the moon is visible
Crescent – only a small portion of the moon is visible
New – the moon is not visible at all

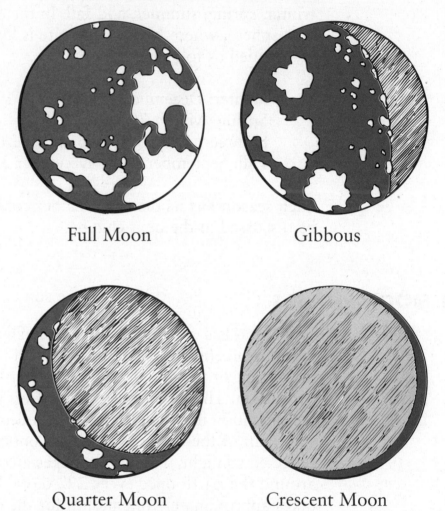

Full Moon   Gibbous

Quarter Moon   Crescent Moon

Because the moon and Earth are constantly moving it is possible for each to move into the shadow created by the other. When one celestial body moves into the shadow of another the event is known as an **eclipse**. There are two types of eclipses involving the sun, moon, and Earth.

▪ **Lunar Eclipse** – occurs when the Earth comes between the sun and a full moon. During a lunar eclipse, the moon appears to be a reddish-orange color when viewed from Earth.

- **Solar Eclipse** – occurs when the moon comes between the sun and the Earth. Solar eclipses occur during new moons. The moon blocks the sun's light from reaching Earth; the sky appears to darken as it moves in front of the sun and then lightens as the moon moves away.

TEST YOUR SKILLS

1. The Earth makes a complete rotation on its axis once every
   a. 15 minutes.
   b. 24 hours.
   c. 2 months.
   d. year.

2. The rising and setting of the sun is due to the Earth's
   a. rotation.
   b. revolution.
   c. gravitational force.
   d. magnetism.

3. We are able to see the moon in the sky because the
   a. moon is only visible at night.
   b. Earth's light is reflected off of the moon.
   c. moon gives off light.
   d. sun's light is reflected off of the moon.

4. The day with the shortest number of daylight hours in New York State would occur during what month?
   a. December
   b. June
   c. September
   d. October

5. The moon _____ around the Earth.

 a. grows

 b. revolves

 c. rotates

 d. tilts

6. John looks at the moon one night and is only able to see a very small portion. In what phase is the moon?

 a. quarter

 b. full

 c. crescent

 d. new

7. Day and year, both units of time, are based on the motion of the

 a. stars.

 b. sun.

 c. moon.

 d. Earth.

8. One complete revolution of the moon around the Earth takes approximately one

 a. day.

 b. week.

 c. month.

 d. year.

9. The different phases of the moon as seen from Earth are caused by the

 a. moon's distance from the Earth.

 b. rotation of the moon.

 c. revolution of the moon around the Earth.

 d. tilt of the moon on its axis.

10. Which diagram best represents the full-moon phase as seen from Earth?

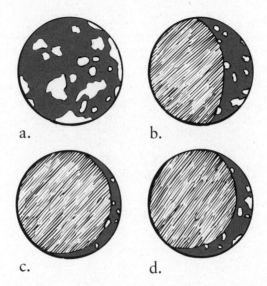

11. The rising and setting of the sun as viewed from Earth is the result of the

a. Earth's rotation.

b. Earth's revolution.

c. sun's rotation.

d. sun's revolution.

12. How long does Earth take to complete one revolution around the sun?

a. 1 day

b. 1 week

c. 1 month

d. 1 year

Chapter 12

WEATHER

Weather describes the conditions in the sky on any particular day. **Climate** describes the weather conditions in an area over time. Weather observations are made using human senses as well a variety of instruments. Some weather instruments include:

- **Barometer** – measures air pressure
- **Anemometer** – measures wind speed
- **Rain Gauge** – measures rainfall
- **Thermometer** – measures temperature

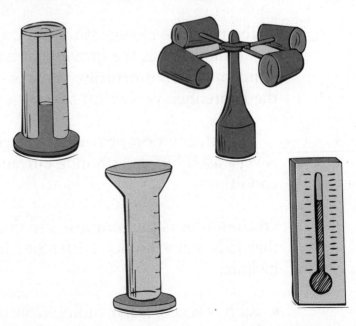

Air pressure is the pressure against the surface of the Earth by the atmosphere. Differences in air pressure over the surface of the Earth result in wind. The greater the differences in air pressures, the stronger the wind. Air pressure is measured with a barometer.

Scientists use an anemometer to determine wind speed. Wind speed is usually measured in miles per hour. A gentle breeze might be measured at a speed of 2 miles per hour whereas the winds from a hurricane could be measured at 100 miles per hour. Wind direction is also important because it can indicate the temperature and moisture level of the wind. A southwest wind would bring warm air to New York from the south, but a northeast wind would most likely bring cold, wet winds.

A rain gauge is used to measure rainfall. The amount of rain that falls can be important in areas that need rainwater for everyday use; especially farmers who need rainwater for their crops. Rainfall amounts are usually measured in inches. The rate at which rain falls can be measured in inches per hour.

Temperature is a measure of how hot or cold the air is. A thermometer is the instrument used to measure temperature. Temperature is measured in degrees on either the Fahrenheit or Celsius scale.

The information provided by these weather instruments is very useful in determining current or future weather conditions.

Precipitation is the term used to describe water (moisture) that falls from the sky. Different forms of precipitation include:

▪ Rain – liquid water falling from the sky
▪ Sleet – freezing rain falling from the sky

- Snow – solid water falling from the sky
- Hail – solid balls of water and dust falling from the sky

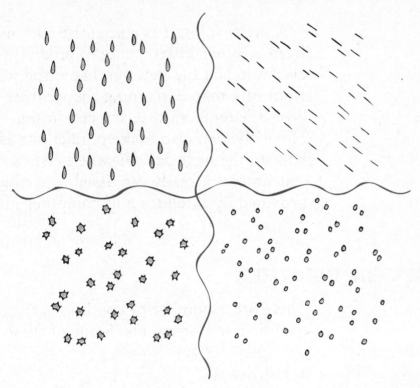

Sleet and snow are more common in the winter months when the temperature is cold enough to freeze water. Hail is commonly associated with thunderstorms in the spring and summer. Rain can occur anytime during the year as long as the outside temperature is above the freezing point of water. Once the outside temperature drops below the freezing point of water it is more likely that the precipitation will be in the form of snow.

Other conditions used to describe the weather include **humidity** and **cloud cover**. Humidity is the amount of moisture in the atmosphere. When the humidity reaches 100 percent it is very likely that some form of precipitation will occur, depending on the temperature. Clouds form when water in the atmosphere condenses on dust particles suspended in the air. Different clouds are associated with different weather conditions. Clouds can block the Earth's ability to absorb light and heat from the sun and therefore can affect temperature.

A **meteorologist** is a scientist who uses the information from weather instruments to predict weather. Have you ever watched the news and seen the weatherperson in front of a map explaining the weather? He or she usually gives the temperature, sky conditions, and precipitation. He or she can also make predictions as to what might happen the next day. Weatherpersons use the simple instruments already discussed as well as information provided by satellites and computer models.

I. SEVERE WEATHER

There are a number of conditions that will result in specific types of storms. Some of these include:

- Hurricane
  - usually occur between June and November
  - very high winds, over 74 miles per hour, and rain
  - develop in the Atlantic Ocean
  - can exist for many days as it moves across water and land

- Tornado
  - can happen at any time of the year, most common in spring and summer
  - usually develop over land
  - have very short lives, seconds to minutes

- Severe Thunderstorms
  - most occur in summer when air is hot and moist
  - lightning, hail, and tornados are associated with these storms

- Floods
  - can occur during periods of heavy rain
  - if the ground is too hard, full of water, or it rains for a long period of time, the ground cannot soak up the water

- Drought
  - occur in areas where there has been little or no rain for a long period of time

These storms/conditions can have a harmful effect on the areas involved. Buildings can be damaged. Crops and vegetation can be damaged or destroyed. Humans and animals can be displaced from their homes and injured.

II. SEASONS/CLIMATE

Each season that occurs in New York state experiences specific climate conditions.

- Spring
  - amount of daylight hours increases throughout the season
  - temperature starts out cold and gradually warms
  - high amounts of rainfall

- Summer
  - longest period of daylight hours occurs at the beginning of the season
  - temperatures get warmer through the month of August

- Fall
  - amount of daylight hours decreases throughout the season
  - temperatures gradually decrease throughout the season

■ Winter
- ■ shortest period of daylight hours occurs at the beginning of the season
- ■ temperatures get colder throughout the season

Because of the tilt and position of the Earth around the sun at different times of the year the two hemispheres experience opposite seasons. For example, when it is winter in the northern hemisphere the southern hemisphere experiences summer.

TEST YOUR SKILLS

1. The weather is part of the daily news. Tracking the weather is most important for people who

   a. work inside banks.

   b. sell televisions.

   c. plant crops.

   d. use computers.

2. Which of these can be caused by heavy rain?

   a. drought

   b. flood

   c. earthquake

   d. volcano

3. Which instrument is used to measure air pressure?

   a. rain gauge

   b. thermometer

   c. barometer

   d. anemometer

4. The term used to describe water that falls from the sky is

   a. temperature.

   b. evaporation.

   c. meteorology.

   d. precipitation.

5. Which of the following is a form of precipitation?

   a. frost

   b. snow

   c. fog

   d. dew

6. A meteorologist is a scientist who

   a. predicts meteor showers.

   b. studies maps.

   c. studies weather.

   d. changes weather.

7. Winds are caused by differences in

   a. rainfall amounts.

   b. temperature.

   c. air pressure.

   d. cloud cover.

Chapter 13

WATER

Water is a substance that is found all over the Earth: in the ground, on the surface, and in the air. Water exists in three phases: **solid, liquid, and gas.**

Water in the solid phase is often called **ice**. Water in the liquid phase is called water. Water in the gaseous phase is often called **water vapor** or **steam.**

Water can easily be changed from one phase to another by the addition or removal of heat. Each phase change that water goes through has a specific name.

Freezing involves changing water from its liquid state to its solid state (ice) by the removal of heat.

Melting is the opposite of freezing and involves changing water from its solid state (ice) to a liquid state by the addition of heat.

Evaporation involves changing water from its liquid state to a gaseous state (vapor). Imagine the puddles that form on your street after a heavy rain. After a few hours or days those puddles disappear. Where did they go? The energy from the sun heated the water and caused it to evaporate—change from liquid water to water vapor. The water vapor then entered the air.

Condensation involves changing water from its gaseous state (vapor) to its liquid state. Think back to a hot summer day, when you poured yourself a glass of cold water and took it outside. After a few minutes water droplets appeared on the outside of your glass. This is because the water vapor in the air came in contact with the cool glass. The water vapor cooled and changed from its gaseous state to a liquid state (droplets) on your glass.

Practice

A. Name the phase change that occurs in each of the following:

    a. ice to liquid water: _____

    b. liquid water to water vapor:_____

    c. water vapor to liquid water:_____

    d. liquid water to ice: _____

B. Liquid water is changed to water vapor by _____ heat.

C. Water vapor is changed to liquid water by _____ heat.

    Precipitation is often defined as water falling from the sky. The water that falls can be in liquid form, such as rain, or in solid form, such as snow. Examples of precipitation include rain, snow, sleet, and hail.

The movement of water between the ground, surface, and air is referred to as the **water cycle**.

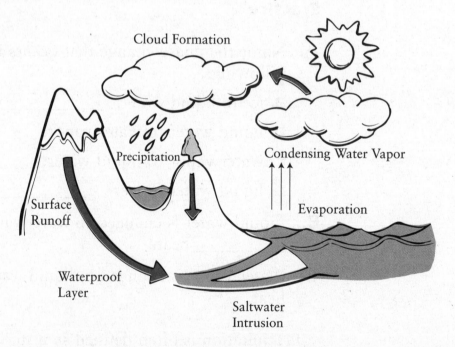

Water found on the surface of the Earth is referred to as **surface water**. Surface water can be **fresh**, such as water found in lakes and rivers, or **salt**, such as water found in oceans or seas. When precipitation falls to the Earth the water is eventually absorbed (taken in) by the ground. Sometimes the precipitation happens too quickly and the ground cannot absorb all of the water. As a result, the water moves across the surface of the ground. Water flowing on the Earth's surface is referred to as **runoff**. When the ground absorbs the water and it settles below the surface it is called **groundwater**.

TEST YOUR SKILLS

1. Which phase change is referred to as condensation?
   a. solid to liquid
   b. liquid to gas (vapor)
   c. liquid to solid
   d. gas (vapor) to liquid

2. Water falling from the sky is called
   a. evaporation.
   b. precipitation.
   c. runoff.
   d. groundwater.

3. The change of water from its liquid phase to its gaseous phase is called
   a. runoff.
   b. precipitation.
   c. evaporation.
   d. condensation.

4. The movement of water between air and land is called
   a. precipitation.
   b. runoff.
   c. condensation.
   d. water cycle.

5. Which of the following is *not* a form a precipitation?
   a. hail
   b. fog
   c. sleet
   d. rain

6. When liquid water changes to water vapor it is called
_____.

7. When water vapor changes to liquid water it is called
_____.

8. When liquid water falls to the Earth from the sky it is
called _____.

9. Describe how water from the oceans enters the
atmosphere.

_____

_____

10. Describe how water from the atmosphere returns to
the rivers and lakes on the surface of the Earth.

_____

_____

Chapter 14

WEATHERING AND EROSION

Weathering, erosion, and deposition result from the interactions between air, land, and water. The processes of weathering and erosion change the landscape of the Earth on a daily basis. Weathering is a process that breaks rocks and other surface materials into small pieces. This can be done through the action of different forces including water and plant life.

Water exists in many phases. Water in the liquid phase often sinks into the cracks between rocks. When the water freezes, it expands, making the crack even larger, and in some cases, breaks the rock. This process continues over long periods of time, breaking down rocks. Plants can also break down rocks by the action of their roots, which are constantly growing to secure the plant and seek water.

As the rocks break, they can be further broken down through continued weathering, eventually becoming very small pieces that combine with other Earth materials to create soil. Soil is composed of pieces of Earth materials, both living and nonliving.

Weathering of rock and landforms can also take place through the action of running water and waves. The flow of water through a landform can create valleys in large rocks. The Grand Canyon in Arizona was created by the flow of the Colorado River over a long period of time. The force of waves breaking on beaches and cliffs can also change landforms.

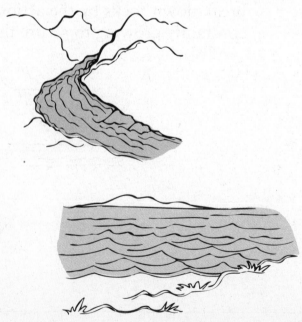

Erosion is the process by which soil and or other Earth materials are moved from one place to another. Water, wind, and gravity are all forces involved in erosion. Examples of erosion include:

- movement of sand along a beach by wave action
- widening of a riverbed by increased water flow

The processes of weathering and erosion work together over time. Rocks are weathered, broken down, and then carried away through the action of erosion. Eventually, the particles that are being moved by water, wind, and/or gravity will stop moving. Deposition occurs when the particles stop moving.

NATURAL EVENTS THAT CHANGE THE LANDSCAPE

Earthquakes are caused by the shifting of the plates that make up the Earth's crust. Earthquakes occur everyday all over Earth. Most of the time people do not feel the earthquakes. However, powerful earthquakes can cause damage to landscapes and buildings.

A **volcano** is a mountain through which hot liquid material from inside the Earth can reach the surface. The hot liquid rock on the surface is called **lava**. Many islands around the world, including the Hawaiian islands, were formed as a result of volcanic action.

TEST YOUR SKILLS

1. Water trapped inside the cracks of rocks may freeze during the winter. This can cause

   a. earthquakes to occur.

   b. rocks to break apart.

   c. diamonds to form.

   d. volcanic rocks to form.

2. Over time, a rock breaks down into small pieces. This is an example of

   a. erosion.

   b. deposition.

   c. precipitation.

   d. weathering.

3. How is weathering different from erosion?

   _____

   _____

PROCESS SKILLS

Chapter 15

PROCESS SKILLS

One of the most useful tools that a scientist has is the power of observation. Simple observations can be made with the five senses: taste, touch, smell, sight, and hearing. The sense of taste is one sense that we typically do not use in a science laboratory or during a science experiment. Scientists often record their observations in a journal or notebook in order to keep accurate records for future review. To help make more detailed observations scientists often use tools.

Tools that a scientist might use include:

- **Ruler** – measures length
- **Meter stick** – measures length
- **Balance** – measures mass
- **Spring scale** – measures weight
- **Thermometer** – measures temperature
- **Microscope** – used to view small objects
- **Hand lens** – used to view objects in more detail
- **Magnet** – detects magnetic properties

Each tool has a specific use and should not be used without proper directions.

Practice

A. What property of an object would you observe when using a balance?

_____

_____

B. What properties of an orange can you observe with your senses?

_____

_____

C. What tool would you use to measure temperature?

_____

_____

I. SCIENTIFIC METHOD

The scientific method is a process by which scientists investigate a problem or situation. The steps of the scientific method follow:

1. Define the problem
2. Research background information
3. Form a hypothesis (educated guess)
4. Experimentation
5. Evaluation

Although the scientific method can be simplified into a series of steps, each step can involve a great deal of work. Once the problem is defined it is important to research information before determining exactly what you wish to study. In some cases the problem can be solved based on the background research; in other cases it is necessary to form a hypothesis. Once a hypothesis is decided upon you can conduct an experiment to prove the hypothesis. After experimentation it will become necessary to evaluate the results to determine whether your hypothesis was correct.

Look at the following problem:

Students wanted to determine if music affected the growth of sunflowers in the classroom. They researched information to find the best soil, nutrients, and light source needed in order to grow sunflowers. One hypothesis was that "Rock music caused sunflowers to grow faster than no music." Students set up an experiment in which they exposed some sunflower seeds to rock music and some to no music. Plant growth was measured every day for two weeks after the first appearance of a seedling. Data was put into a chart and the students concluded that the sunflower plants that were exposed to rock music were taller than the plants that were not exposed to any music.

Practice

D. What is the hypothesis the students were trying to prove?

_____

_____

E. Why did students research the type of soil for the sunflowers?

_____

_____

II. SAFETY

Safety is a very important aspect in the study of science. There are a number of important safety rules to follow every time you are in a science laboratory:

1. Read all directions before beginning a science investigation.
2. Do only those steps described in the instructions or by the teacher.
3. Never work in the laboratory area alone; make sure a teacher is always present.
4. Use proper safety equipment.

   ▪ **Eye Goggles** – protects eyes from chemicals and/or flying objects
   ▪ **Apron** – protects clothing
   ▪ **Gloves** – protects hands/skin from harm

5. Food and drink do not belong in laboratory areas.
6. Immediately report all accidents to the teacher.

Practice

F. Which instrument can be used to measure air temperature?

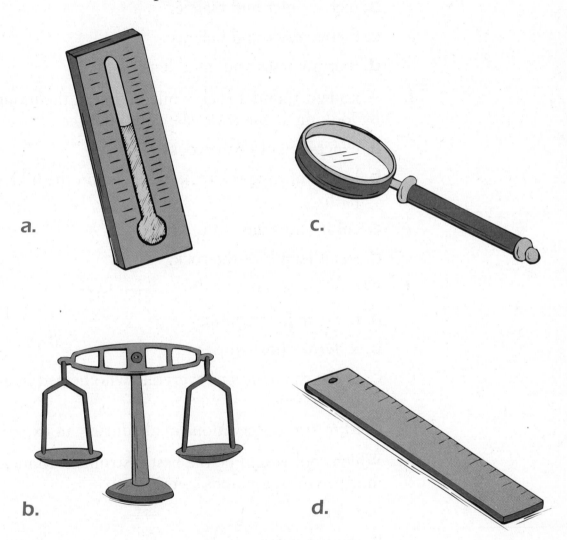

a.

c.

b.

d.

G. A metric ruler can be used to measure the _____

   a. volume of a liquid.

   b. circumference of a circle.

   c. length of a stick.

   d. curve of an oval.

H. Which two tools would help you measure the size and mass of an object?

   a. hand lens and balance.

   b. metric ruler and magnet.

   c. metric ruler and balance.

   d. thermometer and hand lens.

I. A student found a rock while hiking in the mountains. By looking at the rock, she could tell the

   a. exact weight of the rock.

   b. length of time the rock had been on the hiking path.

   c. color and shape of the rock.

   d. exact length of the rock.

J. Why is a journal useful to a scientist?

   a. to write letters home

   b. to write short stories

   c. to list the names of everyone who helped in an experiment

   d. to record observations made during an experiment

K. Which tool would be the best instrument to measure the growth of a plant's stem?

   a. ruler

   b. thermometer

   c. magnifier

   d. cup

L. Look at the chart below. How would you change the chart if you wanted to grow the plants for one more week?

	Plant 1	Plant 2
Height at 1 week	1 centimeter	1 centimeter
Height at 2 weeks	5 centimeters	3 centimeters

    a. add a column for observations

    b. add a column for average height

    c. add a row for soil conditions

    d. add a row for height at 3 weeks

M. The most important safety rule is to

    a. follow all directions.

    b. heat all substances before smelling.

    c. clean all equipment.

    d. mix all chemicals before starting an experiment.

N. Students should wear safety goggles in the laboratory when they are

    a. reading instructions.

    b. drying their hands.

    c. using fire or handling chemicals.

    d. drying glassware.

III. GRAPHING

The graph is a very useful method of displaying data obtained from a number of sources. There are different graphs that you will see and use in your science experiences.

A line graph shows the change in information between two variables. This could be air temperature at different times of the day or the temperature of water as it is heated. The two axes of the line graph are labeled with a description of what they measure and the unit of measure.

The data table might look like this:

Time of Day	Temperature (Celsius)
6 A.M.	25°
10 A.M.	37°
2 P.M.	43°
6 P.M.	32°
10 P.M.	19°

The line graph might look like this:

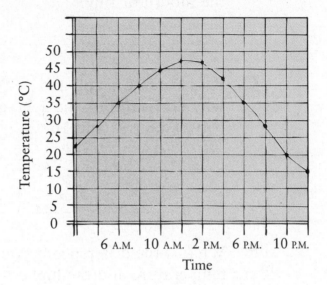

Practice

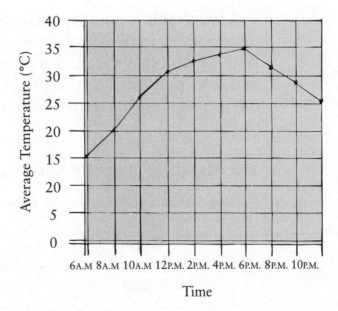

Answer the questions below using the line graph above.

O. What was the average daily temperature at 2 P.M. during the month of July?

P. What was the lowest average daily temperature for the month of July?

_____

Q. Based on the graph and your knowledge of science, why do you think the average temperature decreased between 6 P.M. and 10 P.M.?

_____

_____

R. What is the difference between the lowest average temperature and the highest average temperature in the graph?

_____

A **bar graph** is another form of graph used to present information. In this case the information is shown in the form of bars that are drawn from the x-axis (horizontal axis). A graph such as this might be used to show the number of students with different eye color for your entire class.

The data table might look like this:

Eye Color	Number of Students
Blue	7
Brown	15
Green	4

The bar graph might look like this:

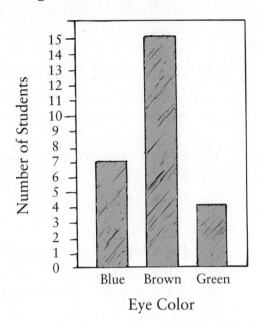

Practice

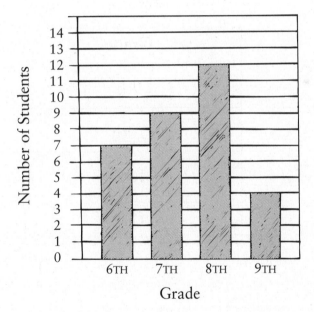

Answer the questions below based on the bar graph above.

S. How many 7th grade students were absent on the day in question?

T. Which grade had the most absences?

_____

U. Which grade had the fewest absences?

_____

V. How many students were absent in both the 6th and 8th grades?

_____

A **pie graph** is often used to show percentages of variables that equal 100. For example, a pie graph can be used to show the percentage of students in each grade in a high school.

The data table might look like this:

Grade	Percentage of Students
9th	40%
10th	30%
11th	20%
12th	10%

The pie graph might look like this:

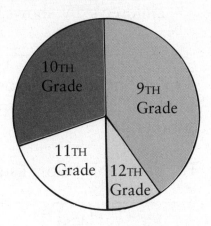

Practice

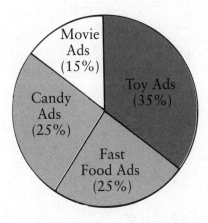

Answer the questions below based on the pie graph above.

W. What percentage of ads shown during children's TV shows were about toys?

_____

X. What percentage of ads shown during children's TV shows were about food?

_____

Y. Which ad type is most commonly shown during children's TV shows?

_____

In addition to the information that we can obtain from graphs, data tables also provide us with a great deal of information.

The data table below lists planets and their diameters.

Planet	Diameter (in miles)
Jupiter	89,000
Mars	4,200
Saturn	74,500
Uranus	30,000

Practice

Use the "Planet" data table to answer the following questions.

Z. Which planet has the largest diameter?

_____

AA. Which two planets are closest in size?

_____ and _____

BB. Which planet has the smallest diameter?

_____

CC. If Earth has a diameter of 15,000 miles, it would be considered approximately half the size of which planet?

_____

A teacher scattered 100 toothpicks of each color on the front lawn of an elementary school. The table below gives information on the colored toothpicks found by three students in a one-minute period.

	Red	Yellow	Green	Blue
Jim	19	20	10	15
Mary	20	18	6	16
Bob	19	16	8	16

DD. How many toothpicks did Mary find in one minute?

_____

EE. Which student found the largest number of red toothpicks?

_____

FF. Green was the color of the least number of toothpicks located by the students. Based on the information provided, why do you think students did not find many green toothpicks?

_____

_____

GG. What is the total number of red toothpicks found in one minute?

_____

The table below gives information on sunrise and sunset times for three days during the month of August.

Date	Sunrise	Sunset
August 15	5:35 A.M.	8:20 P.M.
August 16	5:40 A.M.	8:10 P.M.
August 17	5:45 A.M.	7:55 P.M.

HH. What conclusion can be made about the length of daylight hours for these three days in August?

_____

_____

II. Which date had the most daylight hours?

_____

TEST YOUR SKILLS

Base your answers to questions 1 and 2 on the data table below.

Water Temperature	Average Heart Rate of Water Flea
15°C	140 bpm
25°C	180 bpm
35°C	220 bpm

1. As the temperature of the water increases, what happens to the average heart rate of the water flea?

   a. decreases

   b. increases

   c. remains the same

   d. not enough information

2. What would you predict the average heart rate of the water flea to be if the water temperature were 20°C?

   a. 30 beats per minute

   b. 160 beats per minute

   c. 250 beats per minute

   d. 300 beats per minute

Base your answers to questions 3–5 on the table below:

Water Temperature	Water Depth
21°C	50 m
15°C	100 m
2°C	150 m
–5°C	200 m

3. As the water depth increases, what happens to the water temperature?

_____

_____

4. Why does the water get warmer as it gets closer to the surface?

_____

_____

5. The water temperature at 125 meters would be closest to

a. 15ºC.

b. 13ºC.

c. 8ºC.

d. 2ºC.

Base your answers to questions 6 and 7 on the graph below, which shows the amount of toxic chemicals released in New York State over a period of 10 years.

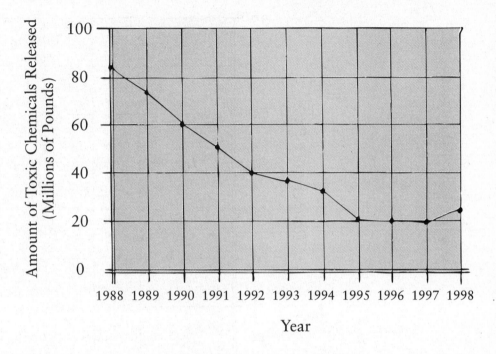

6. How many million pounds of chemicals were released in 1990?

   a. 37 million pounds

   b. 80 million pounds

   c. 40 million pounds

   d. 60 million pounds

7. Describe two negative effects that toxic chemicals could have on the environment.

_____

_____

Base your answers to questions 8 and 9 on the graph below, which shows air temperatures on a summer day in two locations.

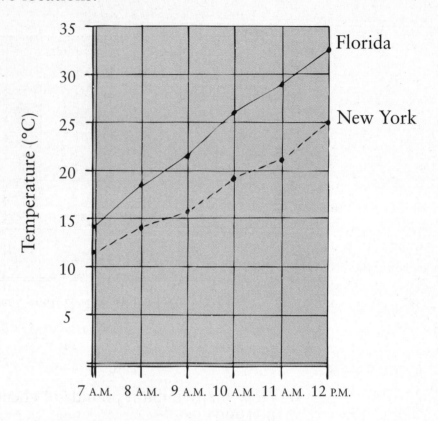

8. At what time of day were the temperatures in the two locations closest?

a. 7 A.M.

b. 9 A.M.

c. 10 A.M.

d. 12 noon

9. At 12 noon what was the temperature in New York?

a. 11°C

b. 15°C

c. 25°C

d. 32°C

Unit 4

PERFORMANCE ASSESSMENTS

Chapter 16

PERFORMANCE ASSESSMENTS

On the day of your performance assessment your classroom will be set up with lab stations. Each student is placed at one of three stations to begin his or her test. The teacher will read the directions to the class. You will most likely enjoy this exam because you will be using scientific equipment and materials to perform different tasks. Each station will have a diagram on the table showing all of the materials you need and how the setup should look. Before you do anything, check that you have all of the materials listed and that the setup is the same as shown in the diagram. When you are told to begin, you will be given 15 minutes to do each activity and answer all of the questions for that station. Be sure to read the directions carefully and relate all of your answers to the activities you just performed. You cannot study for this part of the exam, but you can do some practice activities to help prepare for the performance assessment.

Note: Blank charts for the following activities are at the back of the book.

I. MEASUREMENT

Students will be asked to take the measurements of several substances. They must be able to use a balance, measuring cup, thermometer, and ruler. Students must understand what volume is and know how to find the volume of an irregular-shaped object. The following activities can be modified to where the students take the temperature of different locations in a room or their home and record them in a table.

MEASUREMENT ACTIVITY 1: BASIC MEASURING AND GRAPHING

- **Materials:** ruler and different length objects such as small plastic toys, different length pipe cleaners, and so on
- **Activity:** Use a standard ruler and measure the objects. Organize the objects in size order and record your data.
- **Data Collection:** Develop a table for the object and note how many of each length.

Using a chart like the one below, record your data:

Pipe Cleaner Color	Length Measured
Red	2 inches
Blue	4 inches
Yellow	6 inches
Pink	1 inch

Shade in one box for each inch of that object.

Number of Inches				
6 inches				
5 inches				
4 inches				
3 inches				
2 inches				
1 inch				
	Pink	Red	Blue	Yellow

Pipe Cleaners

■ **Sample Questions:**
  ■ Create a bar graph coloring one block for each inch.
  ■ How many pink pipe cleaners would you need to match the length of a blue pipe cleaner?

___

■ **Alternative Data Collection:** If you were using many different shaped objects:
  ■ Group objects of the same length and create a bar graph using blocks to represent how many objects are the same length.

MEASUREMENT ACTIVITY 2: BALANCE

▪ **Materials:** balance and gram masses (pennies), water, ping pong ball, golf ball, marble, rock, small toy, and so on

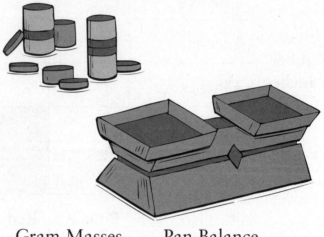

Gram Masses   Pan Balance

▪ **Activity:** Using the pan balance and gram masses (or pennies) students should weigh each object and enter it into a table.

▪ **Data Collection:** Fill in the table.

Object	Mass/Weight Grams or Number of Pennies
Small Rock	
Golf Ball	
Ping Pong Ball	
Small Toy	

▪ Sample Question:
  ▪ What conclusions can be drawn from your results?

_____

_____

MEASUREMENT ACTIVITY 3: VOLUME OF IRREGULAR-SHAPED OBJECTS

▪ Materials: measuring cup, different size marbles, golf ball, ping pong ball, and so on
▪ Activity: Fill a small measuring cup with enough water to cover the largest object if it were placed in the cup.
  ▪ Start with the cup and only water; record amount
  ▪ Place object in cup with the water; record amount
  ▪ Subtract the two amounts to find the volume

▪ Data Collection: Fill in the table.

Object	Water (in milliliters)	Water and Object (in milliliters)	Difference = Volume of Object (in milliliters)
Large Marble			
Small Marble			
Golf Ball			
Ping Pong Ball			

- Sample Questions:
  - What conclusions can be drawn from your results?

  _____

  _____

  - Make a comparison of each object's volume.

II. CLASSIFICATION/SORTING:

Students will sort items by their properties.

- **Materials:** collection of different types of pasta, shoes, buttons, toy animals, fruits, vegetables, and so on
- **Activity:** Use the sorting chart to separate items into groups that relate to specific characteristics for each item. Students should be able to draw a conclusion after sorting to three levels.
- **Data Collection:** Fill in the sorting chart.

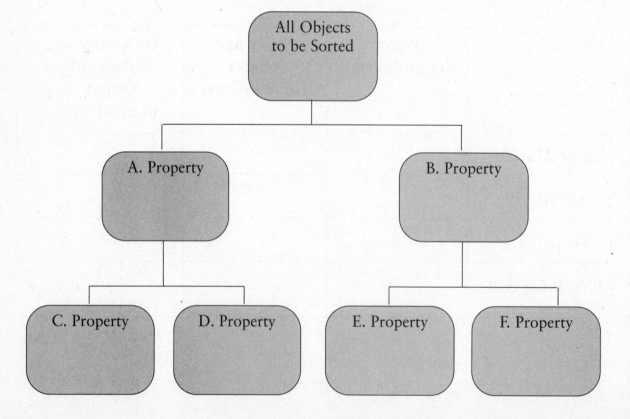

- Examples:
  - **Pasta** – long/short, with lines/without lines, straight/not straight
  - **Buttons** – number of holes: 4/less than 4, large/small, multicolored/solid
  - **Shoes** – with laces/without laces, sneakers/not sneakers, multicolored/solid

- Sample Questions:
  - Give a common name for the objects being sorted.
  - Give the properties for each box in the sorting chart.

    Box A: _____

    Box B: _____

    Box C: _____

    Box D: _____

    Box E: _____

    Box F: _____

  - Which groups of objects are related to each other?

    _____

    _____

III. MAGNETISM

Students will test objects for their magnetic behavior. They will create a table with two columns: "Magnetic" and "Not Magnetic."

- Materials: magnet, collection of common household items such as paper clips, penny, aluminum foil, eraser, toothpick, pencil, plastic toy, metal toy, and so on
- Activity: Test whether each object is attracted to the magnet. If a force is felt from the magnet, the object is magnetic. If no force is felt from the magnet, the object is not magnetic.
- Data Collection: Fill in the table with the objects you used for testing magnetism. Mark an "X" if the object was magnetic or not magnetic.

Objects	Magnetic	Not Magnetic
Aluminum Foil		
Eraser		
Penny		
Pencil		
Plastic Toy		

- Sample Question:
  - What conclusion can be drawn from the objects tested?

_____

_____

IV. ELECTRICITY

Students will use an electrical tester to see whether common household objects can conduct electricity.

The diagram below shows how a simple circuit works. When electrons are able to travel in a complete circle the light bulb will light up. Objects that conduct electricity will allow the electrons to pass when they are put in the path of the wires. If an object is not able to conduct electricity the light bulb will not light up.

- **Materials:** three insulated wires, one D-cell battery, one flashbulb light and holder, collection of common household items such as a rubber band, aluminum foil, penny, magnet, copper wire, pipe cleaner, and so on.

Touch the two wires together to check that the bulb lights up and prove that the electrical tester is working.

Touch object with the ends of both wires.

- **Activity:** Using the electrical tester, test common household items to determine which objects conduct electricity.

▪ **Data Collection:** Fill in the table with the objects tested by the electrical tester. Mark an "X" if the object conducted electricity or did not conduct electricity.

Objects	Conducts Electricity	Does Not Conduct Electricity
Aluminum Foil		
Pipe Cleaner		
Penny		
Pencil		
Metal on Pencil		

▪ **Sample Questions:**
  ▪ What conclusions can be drawn from the objects tested?

  _____

  _____

  ▪ How can you check that the electrical tester is working?

  _____

  _____

  ▪ Explain how electricity travels.

  _____

  _____

V. INCLINED PLANES

Students will send objects down an inclined plane/ramp and note the traveled distance. Following several trials of objects going down the ramp students will record their data, draw conclusions, and make predictions as to what would happen if the objects were released from other locations on the ramp.

- **Materials:** Yardstick taped to a board, toy cars (find cars with different weights), tennis balls, lacrosse ball, hand ball, and so on.
  - For a smaller scale use a foot-long plastic ruler, different size marbles, ping pong ball, and golf ball. Have the balls travel into a plastic cup and mark the distance the cup travels.

Inclined Plane Activity 1: Set the inclined plane or ruler on an angle. This can be achieved by leaning the inclined plane on a pile of books, a small box, or a block. Students should launch the objects from different starting points along the ramp. Test each starting point at least three times.

- The larger setup can be done in a hallway. Use a long tape measure to mark how far the objects travel. The smaller scale version can be done on a desktop or table.

▪ **Data Collection:** Record the distance that the object traveled from each starting location. Enter the data into the table.

Release Point	Trail 1	Trail 2	Trail 3
25 centimeters			
20 centimeters			
10 centimeters			
5 centimeters			

▪ **Sample Questions:**
   ▪ What conclusions can be drawn from this experiment?

   _____

   _____

   ▪ Make predictions as to how far objects would travel if they were launched from a point that is higher than the ruler.

   _____

   _____

Inclined Plane Activity 2: Using the same hallway setup, test objects of different weights from the same launch point on the ramp and make comparisons.

Objects All Released From ___ Centimeters	Trail 1	Trail 2	Trail 3
Tennis Ball			
Lacrosse Ball			
Ping Pong Ball			
Golf Ball			

- Sample Questions:
  - What conclusions can be drawn from this experiment?

  _____

  _____

  - Note the similarities and differences in how far the balls traveled.
  - Make predictions as to how far the balls would travel if they were launched from different starting points. If time allows, students can test their predictions.

  _____

  _____

FINDING THE CORE CURRICULUM AND ASSESSMENTS ON-LINE

To find the Core Curriculum and Standards referenced in this text you can go to the following:

http://www.emsc.nysed.gov/ciai/mst/pub/elecoresci.pdf

To print out the most recent versions of the written exams go to the following:

Spring 2007, May 2006, and May 2005 exams
http://www.nysedregents.org/testing/sciei/science4.html

Click on ongoing archives for the May 2004 exam or go to http://www.nysedregents.org/testing/sciei/gr4elstestmay04.pdf

You can also print out the scoring key and rating guide to calculate your grades.

Please note that the performance test is not available on-line and cannot be released.

Translated exams are also available for Spanish, Chinese, and Haitian Creole.

Other interesting helpful resources can be found at:

www.emsc.nysed.gov/osa
Center Column under Elem/Interm
Go to Science links

GLOSSARY

Adaptation Organism's ability to adjust to its surroundings

Anemometer Instrument used to measure wind speed

Barometer Instrument used to measure air pressure

Buoyancy Ability of an object to float in either air or water

Camouflage Coloring of an animal to blend into its environment

Cell Basic unit of all living things

Circuit Path of an electric current

Classification Organization of matter based on properties

Climate Description of weather conditions over time

Condensation Change of phase from gas (vapor) to liquid

Consumer Organism that cannot produce its own food and must feed on others organisms

Decomposer Organism that breaks down dead organisms and recycles nutrients back into the environment

Digestion Breaking down of nutrients

DNA Stores genetic information

Ecology Study of living organisms and their environment

Ecosystem Living and nonliving organisms in an environment

Egestion Elimination of undigested food waste

Energy Ability to do work

Erosion Movement of materials from one location to another

Evaporation Change of phase from liquid to gas (vapor)

Family Tree Shows how members of a family are related

Food Chain Shows how energy is passed from one organism to the next

Freezing Change of phase from liquid to solid

Friction Force that provides resistance whenever two surfaces are in contact

Genes Structures that carry an individual's traits

Genetics Branch of science that deals with heredity and passing on traits from one generation to the next

Gravity Force that pulls an object toward the center of the Earth

Ground Water Water than moves downward toward the ground

Growth Process by which an organism increases in size

Hibernation State of inactivity; animal's metabolism tends to slow down during winter months

Ingestion Taking in of nutrients

Inheritance Passing on of traits from parent to offspring

Kinetic Energy Energy of motion

Life Cycle Different stages in the life of an organism

Life Span Length of time an organism is alive from birth to death

Mass Amount of material in an object

Matter Anything that has mass and takes up space

Melting Change of phase from solid to liquid

Metamorphosis Process by which an organism undergoes a change during its life cycle

Migration Movement from one location to another, often with change of seasons

Nutrients Materials needed for survival of living organisms (food, vitamins, minerals)

Organ Different tissues working together with a common function

Organ System Group of organs working together with a common function

Organism Multiple organ systems working together with a common function

Photosynthesis Process by which plants make their own food

Pistil Female reproductive organ of a plant

Pollutant Any substance that can harm the environment

Potential Energy Stored energy

Precipitation Describes water falling from the sky in different forms

Predator An organism that survives by hunting and eating other organisms

Prey An animal that may be killed and/or eaten by another animal

Producer Organism that uses the Sun's energy to produce food

Revolution The movement of one object around another, fixed object

Rotation An object spinning on its axis

Runoff Water flowing on Earth's surface

Stamen Male reproductive organ of a plant

Thermometer Instrument used to measure temperature

Tissue Group of cells working together with a common function

Trait Characteristic passed on from parent to offspring

Volume Amount of space an object occupies

Water Cycle Movement of water between ground, surface, and air

Weather Description of the sky conditions at any particular time

Weathering Process by which rocks and other materials are broken down into smaller pieces

ANSWER KEY

PRACTICE AND TEST YOUR SKILL QUESTIONS

CHAPTER 1: LIVING VS. NONLIVING

Practice

A. Three things that you need to live and survive are air, water, and food.

B. Nonliving things that are circled in the diagram: tire swing, ropes, drink, and air. Living things marked with an "X" in the diagram: children and plants.

C. (d) Water helps living things survive by moving materials.

D. (c) Air and water are necessary for both plants and animals to survive.

E. (a) A mountain is a nonliving thing that occurs in nature.

F.

Object	Living	Nonliving
Bench		X
Grass	, X	
Newspaper		X
People	X	
Tree	X	

G. Air and water are two nonliving things that all living things need to survive.

H. **(a)** The life process where animal bones get longer and bigger is called growth.

I. **(b)** The changes frogs and butterflies go through are called metamorphosis.

J. Living things need to take in nutrients so that they can grow and create energy.

K. **(b)** Oxygen is given off by plants and taken in by animals.

L. Fecal wastes are made from unused foods that the animal has eaten.

TEST YOUR SKILLS

1. House – nonliving;
   Dog – living;
   Flowers – living;
   Mountain – nonliving;
   Butterfly – living;
   Chair – nonliving.

2. Answers will vary. Plants need **air, water, nutrients,** or **light** to grow and survive.

3. **(c)** Nonliving thing can be **man-made.**

4. **(a)** Animals need **air, food, and water** to live and survive.

5. **Plants** are able to make their own food by a process called photosynthesis.

6. A seed growing into a plant is a form of **reproduction.**

7. Answers will vary but must include: All living things need air and water to survive; air and water are nonliving. Plants need light to survive; light is nonliving. Some nutrients can also be considered nonliving.

CHAPTER 2: PLANTS

Practice

A. **(c)** For a plant to live and survive, they require **air, water, light, and nutrients.**

B. Chlorophyll is used for **photosynthesis.**

C. Answers will vary. Plant or plant products can include any three: lettuce, oranges, celery, broccoli, carrots, apples, potatoes, and so on.

D. Answers will vary. Animals can use plants for food; a cow eating grass or a horse eating hay. Animals can use plants for shelter; birds building a nest on tree branches or squirrels living inside a tree trunk.

E. **(a)** The process that plants use to make food is photosynthesis.

F. When plants make food, they give off **oxygen** and **water**.

G. **(b)** The plant gets the energy to go through photosynthesis from **sunlight**.

H. The leaves of the plant absorb carbon dioxide.

I. The roots of the plant take in (absorb) water.

J. The leaves of the plant absorb sunlight.

K. **(d)** The two functions of the roots are to **anchor** and **absorb**.

L. Answers will vary but should include: The stem is the pathway of water and nutrients from the roots to the leaves. The stem also supports the plant.

M. The leaves are the food-making factory of the plant. They contain chlorophyll and are able to move toward the sun to collect light for the plant to perform photosynthesis.

N. The flower helps the plant reproduce because it contains the pollen and eggs. The flower is colorful and has a pleasant scent that attracts birds and insects to help with fertilization.

O. Answers may vary. Examples of some common fruits are apples, oranges, peaches, watermelon, cantaloupe, grapefruit, and so on.

P. Fruit develops around the seed and comes from a flower.

Q. Seeds can be spread by wind, water, birds, and insects. When a fruit is moved by an animal or falls to the ground and breaks open the seeds can fall out and grow into new plants.

R. In the desert – (b) cactus

S. In the tropics – (d) palm trees

T. In a New York City park – (c) leafy tree

U. In the mountains – (a) pine trees

V. Answers will vary. Adaptation examples can include: roses have thorns for protection, cactus hold water to survive in the desert, palm trees have wide leaves to absorb extra sunlight, and so on.

TEST YOUR SKILLS

1. Plants need water, light, air, and food to survive.

2. Plants reproduce by forming seeds from the male (pollen) and female (eggs) cells found in the flower.

3. A fruit can be found near the seeds of a plant; usually in the flower.

4. A plant that lives in the desert might have a large root system to find water deep within the ground. The stems might have a tough outer coating to

prevent the loss of water, and the leaves, if they
have any, might be very large.

5. **(c)** Roots secure the plant in the soil and bring in
    water and nutrients for survival.

6. **(d)** Airplanes are not a common method for the
    dispersal of seeds.

7. **(b)** The typical life cycle of a plant is seed →
    seedling → plant.

8. **(d)** An example of a plant responding to a change
    in its environment is leaves falling off trees in fall.

9. **(a)** The part of a plant that is responsible for
    reproduction is the flower.

10. **(d)** The stem provides support for the plant.

11. **(b)** The process by which a plant increases in size
    is known as growth.

CHAPTER 3: ANIMALS

Practice

A. Digestive: take in nutrients
    Respiratory: breathing
    Circulatory: pumps blood
    Locomotion: movement
    Urinary: eliminate chemical waste
    Nervous: senses

B. **(c)** The five senses are controlled by the nervous
    system.

C. **(a)** Animals need air, water, and food to survive.

D. **(b)** Cells → tissues → organs → organ systems →
    organisms

E. **(c)** The mouth helps in digestion and respiration.

F. **(b)** The urinary system is responsible for getting rid of chemical waste and water.

G. **(d)** The locomotion system protects the organs and provides structure for the body.

H. All animals have different structures that have different jobs or functions to help in growth, survival, and reproduction.

I. Answers will vary. Ways that animals respond to changes in their environment, such as seasonal changes include:

Hibernation – going into a dormant state for the winter
Migration – moving to warmer climates
Thick Fur – grown in winter to keep animal warm
Body Fat – increases in winter to keep animal warm
Shiver – shaking to keep body warm

J. **(d)** When animals move to a warmer climate to avoid the change in seasons, we call this migration.

K. **(a)** Some animals prepare for the long winter by going into hibernation.

L. Answers will vary. Students should discuss how dogs have legs, birds have wings, and fish have fins to help them move.

M. **(d)** Some animals have claws, spines, shells, or give off a smell as a defense mechanism.

N. Animals that change color or are of a color similar to their environment can camouflage themselves so that they cannot be easily seen.

O. (a) A giraffe's long neck is a trait that can be considered an adaptation.

P. Pelicans swoop into the water and are able to collect many fish in their large beaks.

Q. (d) The environment that animals with gills live in is water.

R. Answers will vary. Students should discuss how a fish has a flipper or fin that helps them swim. Birds have wings that are long and angled to help them fly. Horses have strong legs and hooves that enable them to run on many different landscapes.

S. (c) Cats' distinct colors and patterns are an example of diversity.

T. The major stages in the life cycle of humans are:

Baby → toddler → child → teenager → adult → elderly

U. The life cycle continues through reproduction and development.

V. (b) Frogs are able to swim with the help of a tail during the tadpole phase.

W. (a) The length of time from an animal's birth until its death is called its life span.

X. Answers will vary. Students can discuss how the ladybug and the frog both start as eggs and go through metamorphosis. The tadpole swims and the frog matures to a land animal. The ladybug grows from a larva that crawls to a ladybug that can fly.

TEST YOUR SKILLS

1. **(d)** The diagram shows the locomotion organ system.

2. **(a)** A defense mechanism is a way in which animals protect themselves.

3. **(b)** Rabbits grow into adults; they have bones that grow.

4. **(c)** Baby → child → adult → elderly

5. **(b)** Reproduction is most important for the survival of a species.

6. **(c)** A bear's fur would be thickest during winter.

7. Answers will vary. Since the dolphin swims its flipper has adapted so that it can act as a paddle. The human uses its fingers and arms for many tasks.

8. **(a)** The brain and spinal cord are part of the nervous system.

9. The four senses that can be used to observe an orange are: sight, smell, touch, and taste.

CHAPTER 4: GENETICS

Practice

A. **(b)** When organisms pass on characteristics from parent to offspring it is called inheritance.

B. **(a)** Characteristics that are passed from a parent to child are called traits.

C. **(c)** A baby can inherit a trait from a parent.

D. Answers will vary. Some traits that can be inherited are color of hair, skin, eyes; height; shape of face, ears, and nose; color of flowers; shape of leaves; shape and color of seeds.

E. Answers will vary. Note that parents are circled separate from child and separate from grandparents.

F. Organisms reproduce DNA from the **parents**, combined to form the genetic information for the new offspring.

G. DNA is like a fingerprint because it is different from all others.

H. **(b)** Genes are found in cells.

I. DNA looks like a twisted ladder.

J. **(a)** Genes carry traits.

K. **(d)** Plants and **animals** closely resemble their parents and other individuals in their species because of DNA.

L. Answers will vary. Answers may include height, color (flower, hair, eyes), and/or shape (leaves, face, ears).

M.

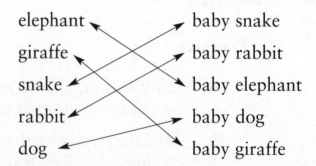

N. DNA is found in the **cells** of our body.

O. DNA is responsible for **telling our body** what to look **like** or can give the body information.

P. All living things have DNA.

Q. Rolling your tongue is inherited.

R. (c) Scars are not inherited.

TEST YOUR SKILLS

1. (c) DNA are the bundles of chemicals in our body that control what we look like.

2. (b) Chromosomes contain hundreds of pieces of information.

3. (d) Parents' DNA (parents' genes) are where our genes come from and determine hair, eye, and skin color.

4. (c) DNA is found in the cells of our bodies.

5.

Trait	Inherited	Acquired
Hair color	X	
Scar on elbow		X
Riding a bike		X
Shape of earlobe	X	
Color of flower	X	
Height	X	

6. Traits are passed to offspring through reproduction.

7. **(d)** This family does not look related to the mother and child.

8. **(d)** A giraffe will have a baby giraffe.

9. **(b)** The flowers in the first generation are all the color of one parent.

CHAPTER 5: GOOD HEALTH

TEST YOUR SKILLS

1. In order for humans to grow and be healthy they need to eat healthy foods, exercise, and get regular rest.

2. **(c)** To avoid getting germs and illnesses from other people you should wash your hands frequently.

3. **(d)** A cigarette is a harmful substance.

4. **(b)** The food pyramid shows us which foods make a balanced diet.

5. **(a)** An example of a poor health habit is eating candy for dinner.

CHAPTER 6: ECOLOGY

TEST YOUR SKILLS

1. The sun is the ultimate source of energy for all life and physical cycles on Earth.

2. **(a)** This diagram represents a food web.

3. **(a)** The cactus is a producer.

4. (b) The butterfly is a consumer.

5. (d) The snake is a predator.

6. Answers will vary. Plants depend on the sun for energy, and on the water and soil for nutrients to survive and perform photosynthesis. Animals need plants for food and energy. Plants give off oxygen for animals to breathe in. Animals give off carbon dioxide for plants to take in. Humans need plant and animals for nutrition. Some animals use nonliving materials for shelter.

7. Answers will vary.
Grass → rabbit → bird
Grass → fly → frog → snake
Tree → squirrel → bird
Water Plant → fish → snake → bird

8. A bird or snake is a predator.

9. A rabbit, frog, or fish is a prey.

10. Answers will vary. Parental care results in better chances of the young surviving. Water animals produce very large numbers of eggs because there are very few young that survive. Animals that do not have parental care have less success in survival.

CHAPTER 7: HUMANS AND THEIR ENVIRONMENT

TEST YOUR SKILLS

1. (a) Humans are dependent upon their environment for food, shelter, and energy.

2. (b) Cars and trucks create gases that are harmful to the atmosphere.

3. Answers will vary. Humans can help save their environment by recycling, planting trees, preventing litter, limiting use of cars, creating new forms of energy, and conserving energy.

4. **(d)** Pollution is created from **harmful gases**.

5. Answers will vary. Harm to the environment can be caused when animals are displaced and the landscape is changed; water runoff, pollution, and so on.

CHAPTER 8: MATTER

Practice

A. In a glass of water that contains ice cubes we find two phases of matter: liquid and solid.

B. Answers will vary. The five senses are sight, smell, taste, touch, and hearing. Students can give descriptions of touching or seeing an object and so on.

C. To determine the volume of this book you would use a ruler.

D. To determine the volume of milk used in a recipe you would use a graduated cylinder.

E. The physical properties of this book are color, size, and shape.

F. Answers will vary. Examples of chemical properties could be souring of milk, the ability to burn in the presence of oxygen, and so on.

G. Answers will vary. The groceries could be divided into a variety of groups: liquid substances and solid substances; edible substances and non-edible substances; colored substances and white substances.

H. Physical properties of the pencil include: yellow cylindrical shape, light, pointy, and so on. Physical changes might include: breaking the pencil into pieces, sharpening the pencil, coloring the pencil with a marker, and so on.

TEST YOUR SKILLS

1. **(c)** A scientist would use a graduated cylinder to measure the volume of a liquid.

2. **(b)** Rusting is an example of a chemical property.

3. **(c)** The particles of matter have the most definite shape in the solid phase.

4. **(c)** Using your eyes to see that a banana is yellow is an example of using your senses to make an observation.

5. **(a)** A balance measures mass.

6. **(d)** Melting of ice is a physical change, not a chemical change.

7. **(a)** The gas phase of matter will take the shape of a closed container.

CHAPTER 9: ENERGY

Practice

A. Parked car: potential energy

B. Bike rolling downhill: kinetic energy

C. Plane flying: kinetic energy

D. Snowball melting in your hand: heat energy

E. Turning on a radio: electricity energy

F. Banging a drum: mechanical energy

G. Pounding a fist on a table: mechanical to sound

H. Drying clothes in a clothes dryer: electrical to heat

I. Battery: chemical to electrical

J. Playing a guitar: mechanical to sound

K. Blender: electrical to mechanical

L. Car engine: chemical to mechanical

TEST YOUR SKILLS

1. (d) A ball rolling down a hill is an example of kinetic energy.

2. (a) Energy from the sun is called solar energy.

3. (b) The energy transformation that occurs when you ring a doorbell is electrical to sound.

4. Energy of motion is kinetic energy.

5. Stored energy is called potential energy.

CHAPTER 10: FORCES

TEST YOUR SKILLS

1. **(c)** This picture represents an inclined plane.

2. **(b)** Friction is the force that slows down or stops the motion of a bicycle.

3. **(c)** A ramp with a low incline would be easiest for Matthew to climb.

4. **(d)** The seesaw in a playground is an example of a lever.

5. **(b)** The only factor that would effect the force needed to move the chair is the weight of the chair.

6. **(c)** Gravity is the force that brings objects toward the Earth.

7. **(d)** If the object is moving away from the magnet then it is most likely another magnet.

8. **(a)** Amanda should use a lever to open the box.

9. **(b)** If an object moves toward a magnet it is attracted to the magnet.

10. A push or a pull is called a force.

11. When two objects slide over one another friction can occur.

12. Objects attracted by magnet: staple, iron nail, and pin.

13. Answers will vary. One conclusion is that metal objects are attracted to a magnet. Another conclusion might be that non-metal objects are not attracted to a magnet.

14. Answers will vary. Students might choose metal objects such as a key or a paper clip.

15. As magnet A is moved toward magnet B you will feel a force trying to keep them apart.

CHAPTER 11: ASTRONOMY

TEST YOUR SKILLS

1. **(b)** The Earth makes a complete rotation on its axis once every 24 hours.

2. **(a)** The rising and setting of the sun is due to the Earth's rotation.

3. **(d)** We are able to see the moon in the sky because the sun's light is reflected off of the moon.

4. **(a)** The shortest number of daylight hours in New York State occurs during December.

5. **(b)** The moon revolves around the Earth.

6. **(c)** The phase of moon that is visible to John is the crescent.

7. **(d)** Day and year, both units of time, are based on the motion of the Earth.

8. **(c)** One complete revolution of the moon around the Earth takes approximately one month.

9. **(c)** The different phases of the moon as seen from Earth are caused by the revolution of the moon around the Earth.

10. **(a)** The full moon appears in our sky as a completely lit circle of light.

11. **(a)** The rising and setting of the sun as viewed from Earth is the result of the Earth's rotation.

12. **(d)** The Earth takes one year to completely revolve around the sun.

CHAPTER 12: WEATHER

TEST YOUR SKILLS

1. **(c)** Tracking the weather is most important for people who plant crops.

2. **(b)** A flood can be caused by heavy rain.

3. **(c)** A barometer is used to measure air pressure.

4. **(d)** Precipitation is the term used to describe water falling from the sky.

5. **(b)** Snow is a form of precipitation.

6. **(c)** A meteorologist is a scientist who studies weather.

7. **(c)** Winds are caused by differences in air pressure.

CHAPTER 13: WATER

Practice

A. Name the phase change.
   a. ice to liquid water: melting
   b. liquid water to water vapor: evaporation
   c. water vapor to liquid water: condensation
   d. liquid water to ice: freezing

    B.   Liquid water is changed to water vapor by **adding** heat.

    C.   Water vapor is changed to liquid water by removing heat.

TEST YOUR SKILLS

1. **(d)** Condensation is defined as the phase change from gas (vapor) to liquid.

2. **(b)** Water falling from the sky is called precipitation.

3. **(c)** Evaporation is defined as the change of water from its liquid phase to its gaseous phase.

4. **(d)** The water cycle involves movement of water between air and land.

5. **(b)** Fog is not a form of precipitation.

6. When liquid water changes to water vapor it is called evaporation.

7. When water vapor changes to liquid water it is called condensation.

8. When liquid water falls to the Earth from the sky it is called precipitation.

9. Water from the oceans enters the atmosphere through evaporation. Surface waters are heated by the radiation from the sun, which causes the phase change.

10. Water from the atmosphere returns to the rivers and lakes on the surface of the Earth as the air cools and water molecules condense. When the molecules become too heavy to stay in the air they fall to the ground in the form of precipitation.

CHAPTER 14: WEATHERING AND EROSION

TEST YOUR SKILLS

1. **(b)** Water trapped inside the cracks of rocks may freeze and cause the rocks to break apart.

2. **(d)** Weathering is the process that breaks down rocks into small pieces.

3. Weathering involves the breaking down of a large object into smaller pieces. Erosion involves moving pieces from one location to another.

CHAPTER 15: PROCESS SKILLS

Practice

A. A balance is used to determine the mass of an object.

B. You can observe an orange's color with your sense of sight, its odor with your sense of smell, its texture with your sense of touch, and you can bite into the orange with your sense of taste.

C. The best tool to use to measure temperature is a thermometer.

D. The hypothesis is that rock music will make a sunflower grow faster.

E. Students researched the type of soil so that they could give the sunflowers the best possible growing condition. Then they would know if rock music made the sunflowers grow faster than no music.

F. (a) A thermometer is used to measure air temperature.

G. (c) A metric ruler can be used to measure the length of a stick.

H. (c) A metric ruler and a balance will measure the size and mass of an object.

I. (d) By looking at the rock, the student could tell the exact length of the rock.

J. (d) A journal is useful to a scientist to record observations made during an experiment.

K. (a) The best instrument to measure the growth of a plant's stem is a ruler.

L. (d) To grow the plants for one more week you would add a row for height at 3 weeks.

M. (a) The most important safety rule is to follow all directions.

N. (c) Students should wear safety goggles in the laboratory when they are using fire or handling chemicals.

O. The average daily temperature at 2 P.M. during the month of July was 33°C.

P. The lowest average daily temperature for the month of July was 15°C.

Q. The average temperature between 6 P.M. and 10 P.M. decreased because the sun is setting, which allows for cooling of the atmosphere.

R. The difference between the lowest average temperature and the highest average temperature is 20°C (35°C–15°C).

S. There were 9 students absent.

T. The 8th grade had the most absences.

U. The 9th grade had the fewest absences.

V. There were 19 students (7 + 12) absent in both the 6th and 8th grades.

W. 35% of ads shown during children's TV shows were about toys.

X. 50% of ads shown during children's TV shows were about food.

Y. Toys are the most commonly shown ad type during children's TV shows.

Z. Jupiter has the largest diameter.

AA. Jupiter and Saturn are the planets closest in size.

BB. Mars has the smallest diameter.

CC. Earth would be considered approximately half the size of Uranus.

DD. Mary found 60 toothpicks in one minute.

EE. Mary found the largest number of red toothpicks.

FF. The green toothpicks blended in with the lawn and were more difficult to see than the other colors.

GG. The total number of red toothpicks found in one minute is 58 (19 + 20 + 19).

HH. The length of daylight hours decreases from August 15 to August 17.

II. August 15 (14 hours and 45 minutes) had the most daylight hours.

TEST YOUR SKILLS

1. **(b)** As the water temperature increases, the average water flea heart rate increases.

2. **(b)** If the water temperature were 20°C, the average water flea heart rate would be 160 beats per minute.

3. As the water depth increases, the water temperature decreases.

4. The water gets warmer as it gets closer to the surface because the surface is closer to the sun and the heat from the sun warms the water.

5. **(c)** The water temperature at 125 meters would be closest to 8°C.

6. **(d)** 60 million pounds of chemicals were released in 1990.

7. Answers will vary. Possible answers might include: chemicals could be absorbed by plants and disrupt the food chain; chemicals could get into the water supply and make animals and people sick; chemicals could damage buildings and structures; chemicals could affect an animal or plant's ability to reproduce.

8. **(a)** At 7 A.M. the temperatures in the two locations were closest.

9. **(c)** At 12 noon the temperature in New York was 25°C.

CHAPTER 16: PERFORMANCE ASSESSMENTS

Answers will vary for each activity based on the materials used.

PERFORMANCE ASSESSMENTS CHARTS

MEASUREMENT CHARTS

Objects	Length Measured

	6 inches				
	5 inches				
Number of Inches	4 inches				
	3 inches				
	2 inches				
	1 inch				
		Object 1	Object 2	Object 3	Object 4

Measuring with a Balance

Object	Mass/Weight Grams or Number of Pennies

Volume of Irregular-Shaped Objects

Object	Water (in milliliters)	Water and Object (in milliliters)	Difference = Volume of Object (in milliliters)

SORTING CHART

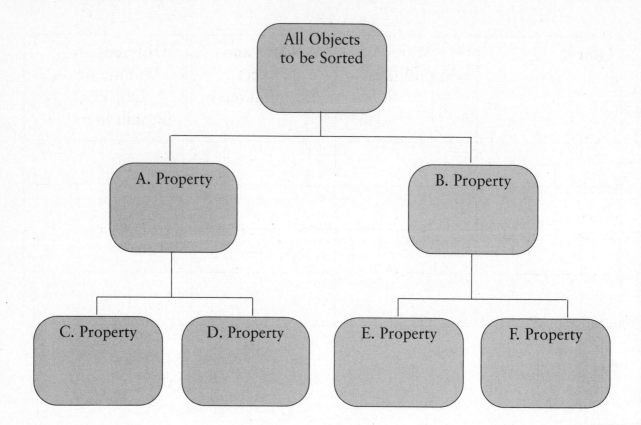

MAGNETISM ACTIVITY

Objects	Magnetic	Not Magnetic

ELECTRICITY ACTIVITY

Objects	Conducts Electricity	Does Not Conduct Electricity

INCLINED PLANE ACTIVITY

Release Point	Trail 1	Trail 2	Trail 3
centimeters			
centimeters			
centimeters			
centimeters			

Objects All Released From __ Centimeters	Trail 1	Trail 2	Trail 3

Unit 5

SAMPLE TESTS

ANSWER SHEET: SAMPLE TEST 1

PART I

1. Ⓐ Ⓑ Ⓒ Ⓓ
2. Ⓐ Ⓑ Ⓒ Ⓓ
3. Ⓐ Ⓑ Ⓒ Ⓓ
4. Ⓐ Ⓑ Ⓒ Ⓓ
5. Ⓐ Ⓑ Ⓒ Ⓓ
6. Ⓐ Ⓑ Ⓒ Ⓓ
7. Ⓐ Ⓑ Ⓒ Ⓓ
8. Ⓐ Ⓑ Ⓒ Ⓓ
9. Ⓐ Ⓑ Ⓒ Ⓓ
10. Ⓐ Ⓑ Ⓒ Ⓓ

11. Ⓐ Ⓑ Ⓒ Ⓓ
12. Ⓐ Ⓑ Ⓒ Ⓓ
13. Ⓐ Ⓑ Ⓒ Ⓓ
14. Ⓐ Ⓑ Ⓒ Ⓓ
15. Ⓐ Ⓑ Ⓒ Ⓓ
16. Ⓐ Ⓑ Ⓒ Ⓓ
17. Ⓐ Ⓑ Ⓒ Ⓓ
18. Ⓐ Ⓑ Ⓒ Ⓓ
19. Ⓐ Ⓑ Ⓒ Ⓓ
20. Ⓐ Ⓑ Ⓒ Ⓓ

21. Ⓐ Ⓑ Ⓒ Ⓓ
22. Ⓐ Ⓑ Ⓒ Ⓓ
23. Ⓐ Ⓑ Ⓒ Ⓓ
24. Ⓐ Ⓑ Ⓒ Ⓓ
25. Ⓐ Ⓑ Ⓒ Ⓓ
26. Ⓐ Ⓑ Ⓒ Ⓓ
27. Ⓐ Ⓑ Ⓒ Ⓓ
28. Ⓐ Ⓑ Ⓒ Ⓓ
29. Ⓐ Ⓑ Ⓒ Ⓓ
30. Ⓐ Ⓑ Ⓒ Ⓓ

PART II

31.

a. _____

_____

b. _____

_____

32.

a. _____

b. _____

33.

a. _____

b. _____

34. _____

35. _____

36.

a. _____   c. _____

b. _____   d. _____

37.

a. _____

b. _____

c. _____

d. _____

38.

a. _____

b. _____

39.

a. _____

b. _____

40. _____

_____

Chapter 17

SAMPLE TEST 1

The test has two parts:

• Part I contains 30 multiple-choice questions.

• Part II consists of 10 open-ended questions.

On the day of the exam, you will have as much time as you need to answer the questions.

PART I: MULTIPLE-CHOICE QUESTIONS

Directions: Fill in the correct choice on the answer sheet.

---

1. Snow and rain are forms of
   a. energy.
   b. evaporation.
   c. precipitation.
   d. clouds.

2. What is the main function of a turtle's shell?

   a. to help the turtle breathe

   b. to protect the turtle

   c. to help the turtle digest food

   d. to promote reproduction

3. Which characteristic is *not* inherited?

   a. how tall you are

   b. having brown eyes

   c. being able to read a book

   d. having blond hair

4. The Earth's main source of energy is the

   a. air

   b. water

   c. sun

   d. moon

5. During which season would a bear hibernate?

   a. summer

   b. fall

   c. spring

   d. winter

6. When you jump up in the air, you come back down to the ground. This happens due to

   a. friction.

   b. gravity.

   c. erosion.

   d. magnetism.

Go On

7. A ramp is a simple machine known as a

   a. pulley.

   b. lever.

   c. inclined plane.

   d. magnet.

8. Which part of the plant takes in water and nutrients?

   a. roots

   b. stem

   c. leaves

   d. flower

9. The tool that is used to measure the volume of a liquid is a

   a. ruler.

   b. balance.

   c. thermometer.

   d. graduated cylinder.

10. Which process results in an animal producing offspring?

   a. digestion

   b. respiration

   c. reproduction

   d. growth

11. A plant in a food chain is called the

   a. producer.

   b. consumer.

   c. decomposer.

   d. energizer.

Go On

12. An example of a poor health habit is

   a. eating candy for dinner.

   b. washing your hands after using the bathroom.

   c. playing at the park every afternoon.

   d. getting 8 hours of sleep at night.

13. Objects being pushed over a smooth surface will move easier due to less

   a. gravity.

   b. mass.

   c. friction.

   d. energy.

14. A rock on top of a mountain is measured at 30 feet high in 1957. Fifty years later, in 2007, the rock is measured again and is now 21 feet high. What term best describes the reason for the rock's change in height?

   a. weathering

   b. wind erosion

   c. water erosion

   d. chemical erosion

15. The force that pulls objects toward the Earth is

   a. magnetism.

   b. gravity.

   c. friction.

   d. light

Go On

16. What force is identified by a north and south pole?

   a. heat

   b. sound

   c. magnetism

   d. gravity

17. Sound waves and light energy are similar because they

   a. move at the same speed.

   b. move by vibrations.

   c. move fastest in solids.

   d. move energy from one place to another.

18. When an object joins two wires and a bulb lights up, the object is able to conduct

   a. magnetism.

   b. gravity.

   c. electricity.

   d. sound.

19. Wind power like that shown in the photo below is a form of

   a. alternative energy.

   b. wasteful energy.

   c. pollution.

   d. fossil fuel.

Go On

20. A simple machine that moves a sail up the mast of a ship is called a(an)

    a. inclined plane.

    b. wedge.

    c. wheel.

    d. pulley.

21. Clouds get their water from

    a. evaporation.

    b. condensation.

    c. precipitation.

    d. perspiration.

22. The length of time from an animal's birth until its death is called its

    a. life span.

    b. instinct.

    c. life cycle.

    d. development.

23. Living things need which of the following to survive?

    a. food and electricity

    b. air, food, and shelter

    c. water, food, and clothes

    d. food, water, and air

24. Which substance is found in nature as a solid, liquid, and gas?

    a. wood

    b. rocks

    c. water

    d. metal

Go On

25. To change an object from a solid to a liquid you must

   a. increase the temperature.

   b. decrease the temperature.

   c. increase the volume.

   d. decrease the volume.

26. When you turn on your television, electrical energy is transferred into

   a. sound and chemical energy.

   b. chemical and light energy.

   c. sound and light energy.

   d. heat and sound energy.

27. A thermometer is used to measure

   a. sound energy.

   b. heat energy.

   c. light energy.

   d. electrical energy.

28. Which part of the plant is responsible for the production of seeds?

   a. flower

   b. leaves

   c. stem

   d. roots

29. Photosynthesis takes place in which part of the plant?

   a. flower

   b. leaves

   c. stem

   d. roots

Go On

30. The people shown below represent three _____ of a family.

   a. versions

   b. generations

   c. offspring

   d. levels

Go On

PART II: OPEN-ENDED QUESTIONS

Directions: Write your answers on the answer sheet.

31. Experimental Observation

Plant A   Plant B

Plant A was placed in a closet for one week. Plant B was placed on a sunny windowsill for one week. Based on this information and what the plants look like at the end of the week, answer the following questions.

a. What was being tested in this experiment?

b. What observation can be made from this information?

Go On

Base your answers to questions 32 and 33 on the drawing shown below.

32. Identify two living things in this environment.

33. Identify two nonliving things in this environment.

Base your answers to questions 34–36 on the food chain shown below and on your knowledge of science.

Go On

34. Which organism is a producer in this food chain?

35. From where does the producer get its energy?

36. Which organisms are consumers in this food chain?

37. Write the tool used to measure each of the following.

Property/unit	Tool
Volume/milliliters	
Length/centimeters	
Temperature/°C	
Mass/grams	

38. Identify two ways the moon is different from the Earth.

39. Identify two ways the moon is similar to the Earth.

40. Thousands of years ago the land in the diagram below was flat. Explain how the canyon was created.

ANSWER SHEET: SAMPLE TEST 2

PART I

1. Ⓐ Ⓑ Ⓒ Ⓓ
2. Ⓐ Ⓑ Ⓒ Ⓓ
3. Ⓐ Ⓑ Ⓒ Ⓓ
4. Ⓐ Ⓑ Ⓒ Ⓓ
5. Ⓐ Ⓑ Ⓒ Ⓓ
6. Ⓐ Ⓑ Ⓒ Ⓓ
7. Ⓐ Ⓑ Ⓒ Ⓓ
8. Ⓐ Ⓑ Ⓒ Ⓓ
9. Ⓐ Ⓑ Ⓒ Ⓓ
10. Ⓐ Ⓑ Ⓒ Ⓓ

11. Ⓐ Ⓑ Ⓒ Ⓓ
12. Ⓐ Ⓑ Ⓒ Ⓓ
13. Ⓐ Ⓑ Ⓒ Ⓓ
14. Ⓐ Ⓑ Ⓒ Ⓓ
15. Ⓐ Ⓑ Ⓒ Ⓓ
16. Ⓐ Ⓑ Ⓒ Ⓓ
17. Ⓐ Ⓑ Ⓒ Ⓓ
18. Ⓐ Ⓑ Ⓒ Ⓓ
19. Ⓐ Ⓑ Ⓒ Ⓓ
20. Ⓐ Ⓑ Ⓒ Ⓓ

21. Ⓐ Ⓑ Ⓒ Ⓓ
22. Ⓐ Ⓑ Ⓒ Ⓓ
23. Ⓐ Ⓑ Ⓒ Ⓓ
24. Ⓐ Ⓑ Ⓒ Ⓓ
25. Ⓐ Ⓑ Ⓒ Ⓓ
26. Ⓐ Ⓑ Ⓒ Ⓓ
27. Ⓐ Ⓑ Ⓒ Ⓓ
28. Ⓐ Ⓑ Ⓒ Ⓓ
29. Ⓐ Ⓑ Ⓒ Ⓓ
30. Ⓐ Ⓑ Ⓒ Ⓓ

PART II

31. _____
32. _____
33. _____

34. _____

_____

35. _____

_____

36.

a. _____

b. _____

c. _____

37.

a. _____

b. _____

38. _____

39. _____

40. _____

SAMPLE TEST 2

The test has two parts:

- Part I contains 30 multiple-choice questions.

- Part II consists of 10 open-ended questions.

On the day of the exam, you will have as much time as you need to answer the questions.

PART I: MULTIPLE-CHOICE QUESTIONS

Directions: Fill in the correct choice on the answer sheet.

1. Which item is *not* a living thing?
   a. rock
   b. grass
   c. worm
   d. rabbit

2. Which is a form of precipitation?

   a. fog

   b. clouds

   c. humidity

   d. hail

3. What is the main source of heat energy on Earth?

   a. fire

   b. volcanoes

   c. the sun

   d. electricity

4. An example of a predator and prey is

   a. rabbit and grass.

   b. plant and sun.

   c. deer and tree bark.

   d. hawk and mouse.

5. The phases of matter are

   a. solid, gel, gas.

   b. gas, liquid, foam.

   c. solid, liquid, gas.

   d. gas, solid, foam.

Go On

6. What type of a simple machine is shown below?

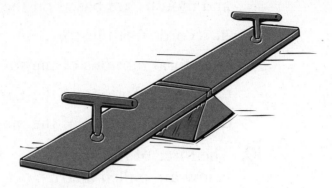

    a. pulley

    b. inclined plane

    c. lever

    d. wheel

7. The position or direction of an object can be changed by applying

    a. force.

    b. magnetism.

    c. chemical energy.

    d. light energy.

8. _____ is a process by which plants and animals increase in size.

    a. Growth

    b. Adaptation

    c. Migration

    d. Variation

Go On

9. Time units, such as seconds, minutes, hours, weeks, and months are based on the

   a. records from history.

   b. natural motions of the sun.

   c. natural motions of the Earth.

   d. natural motions of the moon.

10. The force of magnetism ___ as the magnets shown below are pulled apart.

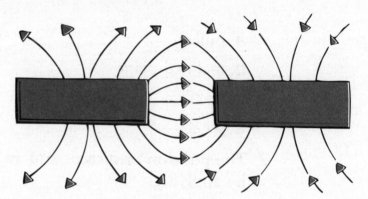

   a. increases

   b. decreases

   c. stays the same

   d. does not exist

11. Which part of the plant is responsible for making food?

   a. flower

   b. leaves

   c. stem

   d. roots

Go On

12. Growth, taking in nutrients, breathing, and reproduction are the

    a. life processes of all living things.

    b. life cycle of living things.

    c. life processes of some living things.

    d. life cycle of plants.

13. An example of the transfer of chemical energy to electrical energy is between

    a. ice and fire.

    b. fire and wood.

    c. sun and plants.

    d. battery and light bulb.

14. An object travels slowly over a bumpy surface and fast over a smooth surface. The difference is due to

    a. mass.

    b. friction.

    c. energy.

    d. magnetism.

15. Some animals prepare for the long winters by storing food and going dormant. This is called

    a. hibernation.

    b. migration.

    c. camouflage.

    d. reservation.

Go On

16. The length of time from an animal's birth until its death is called its

    a. life span.

    b. instinct.

    c. life cycle.

    d. development.

17. Choose the correct life cycle.

    a. baby → elderly → adult → child

    b. child → elderly → baby → adult

    c. baby → child → adult → elderly

    d. elderly → adult → child → baby

18. Why do some animals have claws, spines, shells, or give off a smell?

    a. migration

    b. hibernation

    c. seasonal change

    d. defense mechanism

19. Which is a harmful substance to the human body?

    a. salad

    b. candy

    c. fruit

    d. cigarettes

Go On

20. _____ and _____ closely resemble their parents and other individuals in their species because of their DNA.

    a. Plants, rocks

    b. Animals, rocks

    c. Rocks, insects

    d. Plants, animals

21. _____ is (are) composed of broken down pieces of living and nonliving Earth materials.

    a. Plants

    b. Soil

    c. Animals

    d. The sun

22. What tool would you use to measure the length of a piece of wood?

    a. ruler

    b. balance

    c. thermometer

    d. graduated cylinder

23. Copper wire used to conduct electricity is covered in plastic, which is a(an)

    a. protector.

    b. accelerator.

    c. insulator.

    d. coloring.

Go On

24. Erosion and deposition result from the interaction between

   a. air, water, and land.

   b. water, chemicals, and sun.

   c. air, chemicals, and land.

   d. land, water, and sun.

25. What do we experience on Earth that this astronaut does *not* experience in outer space?

   a. magnetism

   b. force

   c. heat

   d. gravity

Go On

26. How long does it take the moon to circle the Earth?

    a. 1 year

    b. 1 week

    c. 1 month

    d. 4 months

27. Which property of an object affects whether the object sinks or floats?

    a. shape

    b. color

    c. width

    d. weight

28. Color, odor, hardness, and taste are examples of an object's

    a. properties.

    b. mass.

    c. factors.

    d. volume.

Go On

29. What do these animals have in common?

a. same parents

b. same species

c. same name

d. same characteristics

Go On

30. What happens?

a. The circuit is closed and the bulb lights.

b. The circuit is open and the bulb lights.

c. The circuit is closed and the bulb does not light.

d. The circuit is open and the bulb does not light.

Go On

PART II: OPEN-ENDED QUESTIONS

Directions: Write your answers on the answer sheet.

Base your answers to questions 31–33 on the diagram shown below.

31. Identify the producer.

32. Identify the organism that eats the producer.

33. Identify the decomposer.

34. Explain how extreme natural events such as floods, fire, earthquakes, volcanic eruption, hurricanes, and tornados may have a positive or negative impact on living things.

Go On

35. How do scientists make observations?

36. Based on the weather map shown below, list three facts that can be found.

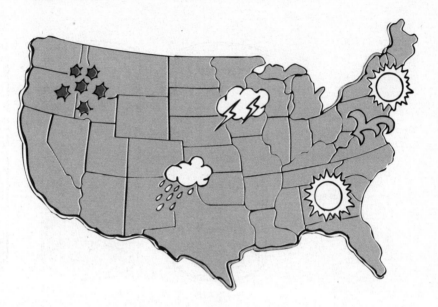

37. Describe two ways that humans can help save the environment.

Base your answers to questions 38–40 on the diagram shown below.

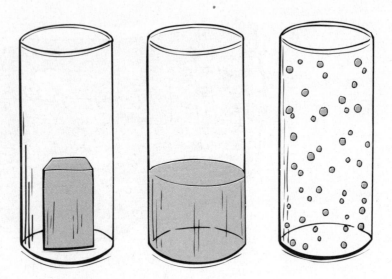

Identify the state of matter and describe the properties for each.

	State of Matter	Properties
38.	_____	_____
39.	_____	_____
40.	_____	_____

ANSWER KEY

CHAPTER 17: SAMPLE TEST 1

PART I: MULTIPLE-CHOICE SOLUTIONS

Question	Answer	Question	Answer	Question	Answer
1	c	11	a	21	a
2	b	12	a	22	a
3	c	13	c	23	d
4	c	14	b	24	c
5	d	15	b	25	a
6	b	16	c	26	c
7	c	17	d	27	b
8	a	18	c	28	a
9	d	19	a	29	b
10	c	20	d	30	b

1. **(c)** Snow and rain are forms of **precipitation**.

2. **(b)** The main function of a turtle's shell is **to protect the turtle**.

3. **(c)** **Being able to read a book** is not an inherited characteristic.

4. **(c)** The Earth's main source of energy is the **sun**.

5. **(d)** A bear would hibernate during the **winter** season.

6. **(b)** When you jump up in the air, you come back down to the ground due to **gravity**.

7. **(c)** A ramp is a simple machine known as an **inclined plane**.

8. **(a)** The **roots** of the plant take in water and nutrients.

9. **(d)** The tool that is used to measure the volume of a liquid is a **graduated cylinder**.

10. **(c)** The process that results in an animal producing offspring is **reproduction**.

11. **(a)** A plant in a food chain is called the **producer**.

12. **(a)** An example of a poor health habit is **eating candy for dinner**.

13. **(c)** Objects being pushed over a smooth surface will move easier due to less **friction**.

14. **(b)** **Wind erosion** best describes the reason for the rock's change in height.

15. **(b)** The force that pulls objects toward the Earth is **gravity**.

16. **(c)** The force identified by a north and south pole is **magnetism**.

17. **(d)** Sound waves and light energy are similar because they **move energy from one place to another.**

18. **(c)** When an object joins two wires and a bulb lights, the object is able to conduct **electricity.**

19. **(a)** Wind power like that shown in the photo is a form of **alternative energy.**

20. **(d)** A simple machine that moves a sail up the mast of a ship is called a **pulley.**

21. **(a)** Clouds get their water from **evaporation.**

22. **(a)** The length of time from an animal's birth until its death is called its **life span.**

23. **(d)** Living things need **food, water, and air** to survive.

24. **(c)** **Water** is found in nature as a solid, liquid, and gas.

25. **(a)** To change an object from a solid to a liquid you must **increase the temperature.**

26. **(c)** When you turn on your television, electrical energy is transferred into **sound and light energy.**

27. **(b)** A thermometer is used to measure **heat energy.**

28. **(a)** The **flower** is the part of the plant responsible for the production of seeds.

29. **(b)** Photosynthesis takes place in the **leaves** of the plant.

30. **(b)** The people represent three **generations** of a family.

PART II: OPEN-ENDED SOLUTIONS

31. Experimental Observation
   a. In this experiment, plant growth, with and without sunlight, was being tested.
   b. Plant A has fewer flowers and looks wilted and unhealthy. Plant B has many flowers and looks strong and healthy.

32. Answers will vary. Two living things in this environment can include trees, people, and grass.

33. Answers will vary. Two nonliving things in this environment can include blanket, basket, thermos, and water.

34. The producer in this food chain is the grasses.

35. The producer gets its energy from the sunlight.

36. The consumers in this food chain are the insect, frog, owl, and hawk.

37.

Property/unit	Tool
Volume/milliliters	Graduated cylinder
Length/centimeters	Ruler
Temperature/°C	Thermometer
Mass/grams	Balance

38. Answers will vary.
Moon: little gravity, small, cold, no real life;
Earth: gravity, large, various temperatures,
supports living things

39. Answers will vary. The moon and Earth are both
round, part of the solar system, and revolve
around the sun.

40. The canyon was created by weathering and
erosion.

CHAPTER 18: SAMPLE TEST 2

PART I: MULTIPLE-CHOICE SOLUTIONS

Question	Answer	Question	Answer	Question	Answer
1	a	11	b	21	b
2	d	12	a	22	a
3	c	13	d	23	c
4	d	14	b	24	a
5	c	15	a	25	d
6	c	16	a	26	c
7	a	17	c	27	d
8	a	18	d	28	a
9	c	19	d	29	b
10	b	20	d	30	b

1. **(a)** A rock is not a living thing.

2. **(d)** Hail is a form of precipitation.

3. **(c)** The main source of heat energy on Earth is the sun.

4. **(d)** An example of a predator and prey is hawk and mouse.

5. **(c)** The phases of matter are solid, liquid, gas.

6. **(c)** The simple machine shown is a lever.

7. **(a)** The position or direction of an object can be changed by applying force.

8. **(a)** Growth is a process by which plants and animals increase in size.

9. **(c)** Time units, such as seconds, minutes, hours, weeks, and months are based on the natural motions of the Earth.

10. **(b)** The force of magnetism decreases as the magnets are pulled apart.

11. **(b)** The leaves are the part of the plant that is responsible for making food.

12. **(a)** Growth, taking in nutrients, breathing, and reproduction are the life processes of all living things.

13. **(d)** An example of the transfer of chemical energy to electrical energy is between battery and light bulb.

14. **(b)** When an object travels slowly over a bumpy surface and fast over a smooth surface the difference is due to friction.

15. **(a)** When some animals prepare for the long winters by storing food and going dormant it is called hibernation.

16. **(a)** The length of time from an animal's birth until its death is called its life span.

17. **(c)** The correct life cycle is baby → child → adult → elderly.

18. **(d)** Some animals have claws, spines, shells, or give off a smell as a defense mechanism.

19. **(d)** Cigarettes are harmful to the human body.

20. **(d)** **Plants** and **animals** closely resemble their parents and other individuals in their species because of their DNA.

21. **(b)** **Soil** is composed of broken down pieces of living and nonliving Earth materials.

22. **(a)** A **ruler** is used to measure the length of a piece of wood.

23. **(c)** Copper wire used to conduct electricity is covered in plastic, which is an **insulator**.

24. **(a)** Erosion and deposition result from the interaction between **air, water, and land**.

25. **(d)** The astronaut does not experience **gravity** while in outer space.

26. **(c)** It takes the moon **1 month** to circle the Earth.

27. **(d)** The property of an object that affects whether the object sinks or floats is its **weight**.

28. **(a)** Color, odor, hardness, and taste are examples of an object's **properties**.

29. **(b)** The animals have the **same species** in common.

30. **(b)** When the switch is pressed down **the circuit is closed and the bulb lights**.

PART II: OPEN-ENDED SOLUTIONS

31. The producer is the grass.

32. The grasshopper eats the producer.

33. The fungi is the decomposer.

34. Answers will vary. Many extreme natural events destroy human and animal homes. A positive impact can occur when a forest burns down and results in new healthy plant life growing from the ashes.

35. Scientists make observations by using their senses: sight, smell, taste, touch, and hearing.

36. Three facts that can found on the map are temperature, type and amount of precipitation, and sky conditions.

37. Humans can help save the environment by recycling, creating alternative forms of energy, conserving fossil fuel, and so on.

38. Solid: holds shape, fixed volume

39. Liquid: shape of container, free surface, fixed volume

40. Gas: shape of container, volume of container

INDEX

Acquired behaviors, 67
Adaptations
  by animals, 45–49
  by plants, 25–27
Air, 19
Air pressure, 138
Alcohol, 75
Anemometer, 137
Animals
  adaptations, 45–49
  basic needs of, 3, 31
  growth of, 52–53
  life cycles of, 49–56
  movement of, 39
  organ systems of, 32–39
  reproduction by, 49–56
  responses to
    environment, 41–45
  structure of, 31–39
  variations, 39–41
Anus, 32
Astronomy
  definition of, 129
  moon phases, 131–133
  time/seasons, 129–131

Bacteria, 74
Balance, 100, 159
Balanced diet, 76

Bar graph, 168–170
Barometer, 137
Beak, 46
Behavior
  acquired, 67
  definition of, 41
  learned, 67
  pattern of, 81
Bladder, 35
Body fat, 42
Breathing, 10

Camouflage, 40
Carbon dioxide, 4, 10, 12
Celestial objects, 129
Cell, 31
Chemical energy, 108, 112
Chemical properties,
  101–103
Chlorophyll, 17
Chloroplasts, 17
Chromosomes, 63
Circuit, 113–114
Circulatory system, 34–35
Classification
  of living things, 3–6
  of nonliving things, 6–8
  physical properties used
    for, 102

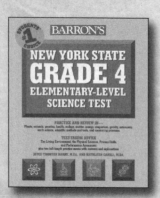